FOOTSTEPS ON THE BACKSTAIRS

FOOTSTEPS ON THE BACKSTAIRS

JOHN BARNES

MICHAEL RUSSELL

© Cynthia Barnes 1992

First published in Great Britain 1992
by Michael Russell (Publishing) Ltd
Wilby Hall, Wilby, Norwich NR16 2JP

Typeset by The Spartan Press Ltd
Lymington, Hampshire
Printed and bound in Great Britain
by Biddles Ltd, Guildford and King's Lynn

All rights reserved
ISBN 0 85955 186 5

Contents

1	Esprit d'Escalier Ecclésiastique	7
2	A Tale of Four Universities	32
3	Wasted Wartime	46
4	Diplomatic Début	58
5	Worm's-Eye View	68
6	London Life: Domestic Drudgery	89
7	Fitful Fifties	106
8	Interest in Israel	120
9	Going Dutch	141
10	Small Talk at Hurstpierpoint	152
	Index	173

I
Esprit d'Escalier Ecclésiastique

Much of my early life and parts of my declining years have been spent on the backstairs of the Church of England. Being born in the Temple, I suppose, set the tone. It is not just the home of lawyers; it has an impeccable ecclesiastical pedigree stretching back through the Crusades to the Old Testament. In Israel it was fun to tell people that I was born in the Temple and watch the double-take.

To my christening, in the Temple Church, the President of the Divorce Court brought a little girl's dress. He, of all people, ought to have known the difference.

The Master's House, designed by Wren or a contemporary, backed on to Fleet Street, so that all the windows faced south and the staircase ran up the solid north wall. The house was bombed in Hitler's war and has since been rebuilt to the same design. We had escaped a similar fate in the First World War; but, as my arrival on the scene more or less coincided with daylight Zeppelin air-raids over central London, my mother and I were removed to the safety of a Redhill villa for months on end. My first Post Office Savings book derives from Redhill; it is many years since the interest has been written up.

I have no memories of the Temple. We did not stay there long. When my brother William was born in 1919, the *Daily Telegraph* ran a headline 'Two little prattlers in the Master's House'. But soon afterwards we were prattling in the precincts of Westminster Abbey. There we really were in the back premises of the church. Our house at No 3 Little Cloisters stood on the site of the infirmary of the medieval monastery and the garden had been the infirmary chapel, for monks who would otherwise infect their brethren in the Abbey itself. The altar step still rose in the middle of the lawn. We felt closely integrated in the life of the whole place; when our pet rabbits disappeared from the garden one day, no doubt for the pot, we were afraid that they would burrow up through the floor of the Sanctuary during evensong.

Although the Dean and Chapter contained some elderly scholars, we

—were not the only children around. Two of them have remained friends to this day: Anthony Storr, the distinguished psychiatrist, son of Archdeacon Vernon Storr, the leading Liberal Evangelical of his day, and Tink Costley-White (now Whitworth), daughter of the Headmaster of Westminster, who became Dean of Gloucester.

Together with them and others, we formed a rentacrowd for the reception of royal visitors. The Unknown Soldier had only recently been placed in his Tomb in the Abbey, and it was *de rigueur* for distinguished foreigners to pay him their respects. Our little party was drawn up on either side of the Tomb and usually attracted some attention. I was indignantly jealous that, while I was only patted on the head by the King of Sweden, my brother was actually embraced by Queen Marie of Romania.

Indeed, at the Abbey we lived in a very royal atmosphere altogether. Not for nothing was it the parish church of the Empire. There was some splendid ceremonial, such as the regular service of the Order of the Bath. But the highlights were two royal weddings, that of Princess Mary to Lord Lascelles in 1922 and of the Duke and Duchess of York in 1923. We were planted in the organ loft, in silk shirts and velveteen shorts, and had a splendid view, right across the Sanctuary to the High Altar, of all the spectacular uniforms and accoutrements. Over fifty years later, I could proudly tell Queen Elizabeth the Queen Mother that I had been a member of the congregation at her marriage, probably one of the last still surviving.

I think there was a telephone at Little Cloisters, hidden under the stairs. But we certainly had no car. My grandparents, too, only drove in two horse-drawn carriages, a Brougham and a Victoria, and continued to do so until they died in 1924. Our daily expeditions were on foot to St James's and Green Parks, with the policeman on point duty holding up the traffic for our nannie, our pram and our dandy dinmont, called Edward because his beard resembled that of his late Majesty. As my mother's parents were still living at Cambridge, we used often to go and stay with them at Peterhouse Lodge and most of our summer holidays were spent with them in rented houses around East Anglia, where we were made to stand up in our pony cart and doff our panama hats if we passed Queen Alexandra in her carriage on the way to Sandringham. On at least one occasion we hired a lorry for the journey and into it we packed the family, our three or four servants, all our luggage, the dog and the parrot in its cage. That parrot, unimaginatively called Polly, was a member of the household for many years; sometime later, it threw a fit one day and my mother hastily revived it with brandy. The fits then became frequent and regular. I have never met another alcoholic parrot. It also caused confusion by calling my mother's maid in my mother's voice.

All too soon, aged five, I had to go to school. This started in Trumpington Street, Cambridge, where I distinguished myself by howling *fortissimo* the whole of the first day. Soon afterwards I was going regularly by 39 bus to Miss Burman's in St Leonard's Terrace, Chelsea. I used to pray for a black fog to give me a day off. My only contemporary with whom I am still in touch is Peter Storrs, nephew of the famous Sir Ronald, who coined the phrase that 'there is no promotion after Jerusalem', a sentiment I was later to come to share. With Peter, too, I attended Madame Vacani's dancing classes, held, I believe, at the house of Mrs David Margesson, with whom I was to stay a quarter of a century later at Kingston in Upper New York State, when she had reverted to her maiden name of Francie Leggett. She was immensely hospitable and gave shelter there to a fascinating mixture of people; but that is another story. Madame Vacani, incidentally, seems to have become an institution rather than an individual; my grandson was going to her classes in the late 1980s.

1924 was a traumatic year too for our family. Almost simultaneously my grandfather Adolphus Ward, died at Cambridge, still in harness as Master of Peterhouse at the age of eighty-six, and my father was appointed to the Bishopric of Birmingham. This meant dismantling two houses and amalgamating their contents into one, luckily much larger, house. Bishop's Croft, Harborne, was only three miles out of the centre of Birmingham, but was blessed with seventeen acres of grounds. It had a Queen Anne central block but two substantial wings had later been added in much the same style and, when the house had been acquired for the Bishop's home, two or three years before our arrival, a chapel had been built on as well.

While the move was on, my brother and I were banished to Exmouth, to make sandcastles on the beach every day. But we were allowed back for my father's consecration in Westminster Abbey on Michaelmas Day, after which we left for Birmingham, where he was to be enthroned in the cathedral on 1 October. In fact, it is only a pro-cathedral, the church of St Philip, designed by Thomas Archer, and boasting only a provost instead of a dean. This was because the see of

Birmingham had only been carved out of the diocese of Worcester twenty years or so earlier. By the same token my father was only the third bishop and, as both his predecessors had been unmarried, the diocese was not used to bishops' wives or children; so at the enthronement we found the cathedral door slammed in our faces and had to parley our way into the ceremony.

The move to Birmingham shifted us on to a quite different plane of existence. In those days bishops were rather grand, wore gaiters and were regularly called 'my Lord'. None of this 'Bishop Ted' stuff. We found ourselves in a large house, with butler and five other indoor servants, two gardeners, a chauffeur and, symbol of status symbols, a car. Admittedly, it was only an Austin 12, a box on wheels, but it could not be more streamlined as my father always had to travel in it in his top hat. My parents did not learn to drive themselves for another ten years or so, instructed by the chauffeur, whose advice on gear-changing was accompanied by such phrases as 'after 'is Lordship 'as performed the hoperation'.

My father was very much the sun round which the lesser luminaries of the diocese revolved and we boys were no doubt snobbishly conscious of his position. But as he was already a pretty notorious figure, we were not easily allowed to forget it. As soon as we went to boarding-school, we were nicknamed Bish and Little Bish. Even so, at home in those days, we really were kept very much on the backstairs. My parents were extremely busy and we were neither much seen nor heard. When we were a bit older, we were expected to attend family prayers, which my father read daily before breakfast in the dining-room. The servants trooped in and knelt before the sideboard with their backs to us. I shall never forget that row of upturned soles. I hope their souls were upturned too. In all my life, I only remember receiving three pieces of advice from my father: always to use a handkerchief when sneezing, always to pour wine in one motion and, when driving, always to beware of the other fool.

Almost the only time I remember receiving any praise from him was soon after the war when we were driving in Devon and had to go through a flood, so that the engine stopped dead. Being recently out of the army I was able to take the carburettor to bits, remove the sandstone, reassemble it and start the car. My father had always told me that I had better learn to maintain a car as I should never be able to afford a chauffeur. I used to remember that when being driven around Holland in a Rolls-Royce.

Moreover the house was rarely empty of guests. At that time the Church of England was riven with factions. When has it not been? There were three main parties. The Anglo-Catholics were the thorns in my father's flesh, on doctrinal and ritualistic grounds. My father was generally allergic to Catholicism. The only Italian saint he was prepared to worship was Santa Siesta. The Evangelicals, except those of the literal persuasion, were also largely hostile to his views on evolution and biblical exegesis. His only supporters were the Modernists. Most Anglo-Catholics would not have been seen dead at Bishop's Croft. Our clerical guests were thus mostly Modernists and Liberal Evangelicals.

Three times a year we had an ordination retreat in the house. Up to ten ordination candidates would assemble and stay from Thursday to Sunday usually under the guidance of one of the examining chaplains, Modernists to a man. We all had meals together, where the atmosphere was strongly reminiscent of the famous *Punch* cartoon of the curate's egg, although I never actually heard one of them say 'good in parts, my Lord'. On the Sunday morning they were all metamorphosed into dog-collars all round the breakfast-table and then trooped off to the cathedral to be deaconed or priested.

But other more distinguished clergy used to come on special occasions. We were into bishops in a big way. William Temple, for example, for the twenty-fifth anniversary of the diocese. He had an immense reputation as a religious leader but at close quarters seemed more like a politician or even a stockbroker. He also had an immense girth: the story of his surplice coming back from the laundry marked 'one bell-tent' is an old chestnut. He kindly seconded me for the Athenaeum and the last time I saw him there was in the urinal, where he was so large that he took up two stalls.

Or there was Hensley Henson, Bishop of Durham. His conversation sparkled like diamonds with epigram and paradox. He was no respecter of persons. I remember him once at dinner complaining that Cosmo Gordon Lang behaved like a heavy uncle to the royal family. Or abusing the young for going to the cinema; 'ruining their eyesight in order to corrupt their morals'.

I never met Lang socially. My father did not like him, quite apart from crossing swords with him professionally. He used to complain that Lang wandered around Lambeth Palace in a purple cassock 'like some petty cardinal' instead of showing the dignity of an Archbishop of Canterbury. A more malicious story was told, not by my father, of Lang, when Archbishop of York, deciding that he needed a wife. So he took his intended for a walk in the grounds of Bishopsthorpe and when they came to a grassy bank took out a handkerchief and spread it on the ground. She thought this a delicate attention to her comfort. Lang sat on it himself. Launching into his proposal for his new state in life, he is thought to have said 'Dear lady, the past is atrophied'. But she was not sure whether he had said 'the parts are atrophied' and decided not to take the risk.

Other, non-episcopal, allies of my father, and frequent visitors, were Dean Inge and Charles Raven. Inge was a national figure, largely because of his witty journalism. It was said that when Beaverbrook first asked him to write in his newspapers, Inge had hoped to escape by demanding what he thought would be a prohibitive fee, but the Beaver had said snap and called his bluff. His views were always incisively expressed; as he said, 'I rhyme with sting and not with cringe'. Staying with us once, he was sent to bed with a who-dun-it; when my mother asked him at breakfast if he had slept well, he snapped 'No, but I finished it'.

Raven was a much less abrasive character. Handsome as a matinée idol, he maintained a youthful charm almost into old age. He used it to great effect in the pulpit, but was also a scholar of no mean ability. He would have liked to write my father's life and my mother would have encouraged him. But I was afraid that he would be too emotional about it. He himself suffered from his biographer, a former Dean of Liverpool, who just sentimentalised his story.

In the 1980s Susan Howatch has produced three blockbuster novels purporting to be based on the careers of Henson, Inge and Raven, but endowing them with lurid sex-lives which would probably have startled her subjects as much as her readers.

But these comments reflect hindsight, not the reactions of a seven-year-old on first arrival in Birmingham. In 1926 I was sent to boarding-school, first to a Dotheboys Hall establishment called Dunchurch, where a pass at Common Entrance was regarded as the acme of achievement, and then, thank goodness, in 1928 to the Dragon School at Oxford, where standards were a good deal higher.

The new departure confronted me with one of the baneful themes of my existence: the importance of not being Ernest. Hitherto I had recognised myself as John; now I became E. J. W. Barnes. My parents had decided to call me John, partly because St John the Baptist's feast day came two days after my birthday and the gospel contained the assertion by Zacharias, 'his name shall be John', a sort of *sors Vergiliana*, and partly because my mother's ancestors had for generations been called John Ward, thus supplying my two middle names. So far, so good. But then, out of respect for my father, they had put his name, Ernest, in front. I can see that, with my father's vague anti-semitism, he might not have wanted me to be J. E. W. Barnes, not that it would have depressed me unduly in later life. Even Siegmund Warburg used to say that I was an honorary Jew. But that initial E has bedevilled me ever since. On admission to Winchester, I was addressed in Latin as 'Erneste'. Even the accolade had to be conferred on 'Sir Ernest John'. Lesser mortals receive short shrift; begging letters using the hated name go straight into the waste-paper basket. But I fear that the struggle naught availeth. I shall never live it down.

Neither Dunchurch nor the Dragon was much into church affairs. At Dunchurch we went to the parish Church on Sunday in Eton collars and black bumfreezers; at the Dragon we conducted the services ourselves in open-necked shirts and short blue trousers. The only bishop I connect with the Dragon was Robert Runcie, who many years later preached at the school's centenary service. He was not a Dragon himself, although his son was. He started his sermon by saying 'I am Bishop of St Alban's and I go round trying to persuade people that the patron saint of England ought to be St Alban rather than St George. This is because I cannot approve of a patron saint who spent his time killing Dragons.' Loud applause.

The Dragon School has been called a forcing-house. Be that as it may three of my Dragon contemporaries, who remained friends into later life, had been honoured by notices in the *Dictionary of National Biography* before 1980: Richard Blackwell, Alastair Buchan and Michael Cary. They all died tragically young. They all had distinguished fathers, but their achievements were independent of their antecedents: Richard as the innovative head of the family bookselling and publishing firm, Alastair as the founder of the Institute of Strategic Studies and the familiar of statesmen around the world, Michael as permanent head of the Ministry of Defence and a maker of harpsichords in his spare time. Another contemporary was

Leonard Cheshire, the only man, I believe, to have both the VC and the OM.

The other feature of the Dragon School, exceptional for its time, was that it was co-educational, at least to the extent of having some 20 girls among over 300 boys. How often have I dined out on the memory of being the only man in the room who has played rugger with a girl in the front row of the scrum.

Winchester, having been founded by a bishop, was much more episcopal, or at least ecclesiastical. I was put in for a scholarship in 1930 and, knowing that I could have another try the next year, was totally relaxed and got in first time. All I can remember of the examination was that we had to translate into French:

> Although of our heroes only Hobbs
> Has made more centuries than blobs,
> Who doubts that England wins the Test
> That tells us where the Ashes rest?

This was no doubt set by Rockley Wilson, the former England cricketer who taught French halfway up the school. I do not know what I wrote, but the school solution started to the effect:

> Quoiqu'il n'y a qu'Hobbs de tous nos héros
> Qui a fait plus de centaines que de zéros . . .

As adolescents we most of us went through a phase of religious mania. Indeed one could hardly help it as we had to attend chapel twice every weekday, three times on Saturdays and four on Sundays. I certainly went through a Modernist phase and an Anglo-Catholic phase, although I cannot remember ever being a biblical fundamentalist Evangelical, still less a charismatic speaking with tongues. Nowadays, I must confess that I find myself more attracted to the ethic than to the magic of Christian theology. No doubt it was all a way of letting off steam, as we were also made to work pretty hard. My first half I was up to the Jacker (which being interpreted means that my form master that first term was Mr Jackson). Having assessed my abilities and knowing that I somehow had a scholarship, he dubbed me 'the miracle of 1930'. Luckily I escaped him after one term, although later on he was very generous to me, as our fathers had been Fellows of Trinity, Cambridge, together. He was rightly very proud of his father, who had been awarded the OM, but probably did not know that his father had been largely instrumental in ousting mine from Trinity in 1915. When our elder son, Simon, went to Winchester, the Jacker was still around and supervised his efforts as Editor of the *Wykehamist*.

But I owed most to three Winchester masters: Budge Firth, Cyril Robinson and John Poynton. Much has been written about Budge. He was in many ways an eighteenth-century figure with a fine sense of history. But he had taken all ten wickets for Winchester against Eton, although it beats me how he did it with his pebble-glasses. He took great trouble to teach us civilised values. In return I persuaded my father to invite him to take one of those ordination retreats. He arrived with a bundle of cigars which he said his own father had given him as a gesture of encouragement, even though he could not share Budge's religious convictions. His father with a long family background of Sheffield steel was a Fleet Street editor. Budge asked me to be an usher at his wedding to Priscilla Woods, daughter of the Bishop of Lichfield. I thought it would be a cushy job with all of Lichfield Cathedral in which to park people. But they had so many guests that by the end we were practically hanging them on the gargoyles. Budge ended up living in our old house as Master of the Temple, and dying much too young.

Cyril Robinson, the 'Bin' as he was known to distinguish him from Malcolm Robertson, the 'Bobber', was the first master to make me realise that work could be interesting, thanks to his own infectious enthusiasm. Until I reached his division, I had sat sulkily in the back row at the feet of some dryasdust pedagogues. I now found that I actually wanted to do better. John Poynton at first sight looked another inhibited grammarian. But this was due to his intense shyness; in fact, he had a delightful sense of humour, usually expressed in topical light verse, alas all too ephemeral. More than anyone else at Winchester, he taught us standards, standards of scholarship and style. His translations into and out of Latin and Greek were of such elegance that we were shamed into trying to emulate him. It brushed off onto our English too. To this day it is thanks to him that I shudder at a split infinitive and many other solecisms.

Both my headmasters at Winchester went on to be bishops, A. T. P. Williams to Durham and Winchester and Spencer Leeson to Peterborough. Williams was a tall, rather remote figure, with a liking for strange phrases like 'mumbo-jumbo', 'Tohu-bohu' or 'mumpsimus-sumpsimus' and a habit, when preaching, of involving himself in subordinate clauses each of which had to be tidily completed, so that one sermon was reputed to end '... has, was, is'. He was the first person I heard define the four stages of drunkenness as: jocose, bellicose, lachrymose and comatose. But he was down to earth enough to give us eminently practical instruction on passing the Divinity exam for School Certificate; perhaps he had set the paper himelf. Some years later, when my father wanted to invite him, as Bishop of Durham, to address the Birmingham Diocesan Conference, precursor of the Synod, his clergy objected that Williams was the dullest bishop on the bench. Yet he had been a triple first at Oxford.

If Williams was transcendent, Leeson was very much immanent. He flung himself with almost indiscriminate enthusiasm into everything he touched and really seemed to take an interest in us as individuals. But he was not infallible. One Sunday in my last year he asked me to dinner. Being well trained I was the first guest to arrive, wondering what was expected of me, as no other boys were present. It soon became clear that I was supposed to know about bishops. After a quarter of an hour or so, Bishop Neville Talbot, who had been a well-known army chaplain, breezed into the room in a purple cassock: 'Sorry, I'm late, Headmaster, I've been drinking beer with Harry Altham' (the cricket master). Leeson took that in his stride. There was then another long wait until the Bishop of Gloucester, Arthur Headlam, an Old Wykehamist, was announced. He was in faultless black episcopal evening dress, silk stockings, buckled shoes, the lot. Leeson, who had obviously expected to see him in purple, greeted him effusively: 'Bishop, I am so glad to see you haven't changed.' 'I have changed,' said Headlam. We then went into dinner and Leeson, rather unwisely with a bishop to right and a bishop to left of him, said 'Bishop, will you say grace?' There was a long silence and eventually the Headmaster muttered grace himself. As we sat down, Headlam pronounced 'I never say grace in other people's houses, even when I am asked to. Every man is a priest in his own house.' The rest of the evening was not a success.

At Cambridge, apart from having to don a surplice from time to time to read the lesson in chapel, I had little to do with the church or churchmen. It was not until 1974 when Bishop John Robinson, of *Honest to God* fame, organised a service to commemorate the centenary of my father's birth, that we found ourselves more involved. Various Fellows of Trinity who had known my father attended, including J. E. Littlewood, the Senior Fellow, then in his nineties, who had been a mathematical pupil of my father and then shared in the great Hardy-Littlewood duumvirate of mathematicians. As he had not graced Trinity Chapel within living memory, a surplice had to be found for him at short notice. We had assembled all my father's living descendants to attend and those of us of years of discretion were invited to dine in hall afterwards. As our daughter Sarah was reading mathematics at Oxford at the time, I arranged for her to sit next to Littlewood in the hope that some knowledge would rub off. When I told this to the Master, Rab Butler, beside whom I was sitting, he asked 'Do you know about Littlewood?' I said that I knew he was one of the two best mathematicians of his generation. 'I daresay', said Rab, 'but before dinner he takes three double vodkas, during dinner three pints of beer and after dinner when the port, madeira and brown sherry come round and you are supposed to take one of them, he takes all three.' Somewhat apprehensively after dinner I asked Sarah how she had got on with Littlewood. 'He taught me to take snuff.' Her mathematics finals did not benefit.

That same autumn of 1974, we went to Birmingham for the fiftieth anniversary of my father's arrival in the diocese as bishop. We were warmly welcomed by the current bishop, Laurence Brown, and his wife, attended a service at the cathedral and a civic reception at the Council House and I slept in my old night nursery at Bishop's Croft fifty years to the day after I had first occupied it. Backstairs again.

Seven years in the army provided a prolonged holiday from ecclesiastical affairs. But when I came back to England in 1946, I had to attend the christening of a new godson. It was held at St Cuthbert's, Philbeach Gardens where the incumbent was Canon Gage Brown and the churchmanship was as high as Everest. The christening was to take place during evensong but that morning there had been a Kensitite raid on the church by the Protestant Truth Society and when some strange young people arrived as godparents, we could see the regular congregation assuming that we were the second wave of the attack and girding their umbrellas to repel boarders. However, the service proceeded undisturbed except that, when the time came for the baptism, the incense was so thick that we could hardly see our way to the font. As we groped along I was about to tell my fellow godfather that I did not know the drill, when he turned to me and said 'You will have to say the responses. I can't because I am a professing Jew.' This was Stormont Mancroft. So to this day I do not know whether that child was effectively baptised.

Shortly after the war I was sent to Washington and there again I had little to do with Church affairs, except that during that time my father published his *Rise of Christianity* and was told by Archbishop Fisher that he ought no longer to be a bishop. I was able to quote to him what Dr Major had said to Bishop Boyd Carpenter on a similar occasion: 'Much patience, but no resignation'. I cannot say that I was one of Fisher's warmest admirers, although I must admit that, after we had both retired and I was asked to remove a critical passage from something I had written for a church magazine, he wrote me a charmingly simple and humble letter of thanks.

One memory of him was when he addressed an Athenaeum talk dinner on 'Crime and Sin'. The proceedings of those dinners are meant to be confidential but perhaps this breach will be forgiven me. Fisher went on about adultery, abortion, artificial insemination, homosexuality and so on, having apparently spent much time at Lambeth counselling people on all these matters. When the debate was thrown open to the floor, Geoffrey Gorer the anthropologist said that, for the Archbishop, sin seemed to be exclusively sexual sin. 'No,' said the Archbishop, rising to his feet, 'I mentioned gambling once.'

On the subject of the Athenaeum it was always supposed to be a haunt of bishops, some of them playing billiards in the basement in their shirtsleeves. There came a time when the club library was losing a great many books, believed stolen. The committee appealed to Sir Robert Watson Watt, inventor of radar, to ask if he could not put a piece of metal into the library books and arrange a radar pulse across the front door, so that it would go 'ping' whenever a member went out with a library book concealed about his person. Sir Robert replied that this would not work as the machine would go 'ping' every time a bishop went through wearing his pectoral cross.

It was not until we went to Beirut in 1952 that we again found ourselves immersed in religious matters with a vengeance. The Lebanon is structured on a variety of religions. Partly this goes back to the Ottoman Empire, which delegated to each religious community, or Milet, the right to administer its own private law, on matters such as property, inheritance, marriage and so on. But partly the position of the various sects is regulated by the National Contract, concluded when the Lebanon became independent, and based on the premise, which only lasted a very short time if it was ever true at all, that the Christian and Moslem communities were numerically equal.

Thus the jobs were shared out. The President of the Republic was always a Maronite Christian, the Speaker of the Parliament a Shi'a Moslem, the Prime Minister a Sunni Moslem, the Foreign Minister a Greek Catholic, the Minister of Defence a Druze and so on down the line. This tended to restrict the craft of cabinet-making, although it did not prevent ambitious politicians changing their religion in order to obtain office. There were sixteen of these milets in all; but, unluckily, the Anglicans, having come on the scene too late, did not qualify. So, although we had our own little church and chaplain, we could not legally solemnise marriages or register births or deaths; these had to remain consular functions. I only remember one wedding in our church when, in the absence of the Ambassador, I had to give the bride away; this went against the grain as she was a very pretty girl and I should have liked to keep her for my own harem. We belonged, incidentally, to the Jerusalem diocese, which then only boasted a bishop, although I was to know it better as an archbishopric in years to come.

Beirut in those days was the only town apart from Rome where there resided more than one cardinal of the Roman Catholic Church. These were Cardinal Tappouni, the Syrian Catholic Patriarch, and Cardinal Agagianian, the Armenian Catholic Patriarch. Tappouni had the reputation of having served French interests faithfully. As Agagianian had lived in Australia and spoke English, the Lebanese, always ready since the days of T. E. Lawrence to suspect the hand of l'intelligence service, naturally assumed, quite unjustly as far as I am aware, that he was a British agent. However that may have been, these two princes of the Church were not on speaking terms. When they both came to the Queen's Birthday party, we had to keep them apart: 'par ici, Eminence' and 'de ce côté-ci, Monseigneur' as we ensured that scarlet silk robes were seen disappearing behind widely separated trees or bushes.

But the chief religious dignitary in the country was the Maronite Patriarch. The then incumbent was aged ninety-four and it was the custom for the British representative to pay an annual call on him. Seeking to do him honour, I took my wife with me, only to discover, when we were ushered into the presence, that he was in bed. At the age of ninety-four, this should have been safe, but it took us a long time to live down this shocking impropriety.

When we went to Bonn, we moved into the diocese of Fulham, a title designed to bring it under the overriding jurisdiction of the Bishop of London, although all its buildings and clergy were on the mainland of

Europe. I was to be much involved in their problems later. But at the time I was delighted to find that for some of those years the Bishop of Fulham was Robert Stopford, with whom I had bathed off Delos on a Hellenic Travellers' cruise in the 1930s. We were to meet again in Israel years later. But the Embassy at Bonn had no Anglican church of our own. For our place of worship we borrowed a little Lutheran chapel, which was so depressing with its sombre black hangings that we preferred to have our children christened in our drawing-room.

Our next venture abroad was to Harvard University where, of course, the writ of the Church of England does not run. But the American Episcopal Church is within the Anglican Communion and we attended its services at Cambridge, Massachusetts. The highlight was a visit by Leonard Wilson, my father's successor as Bishop of Birmingham. He preached a sermon which he had no doubt preached many times before and reduced to a fine art of timing. It was about his experiences as Bishop of Singapore, where he had been taken prisoner by the Japanese and brutally treated. When he described a beating and said, as a throwaway line, 'It was not too bad until they hit the kneecap', there was an audible collective gasp of horror from the whole congregation. The sermon then built up, through his release and restoration to his see, to the climax of his first post-war confirmation, including some prisoners of war, when he saw that one of the candidates kneeling before him was the man who had hit his kneecap. Leonard Wilson had a reputation as a tartar among his own clergy but he was very kind and considerate to me. His daughter, Susan Cole King, who lived near us in Sussex for a time, later went to the USA, where she was ordained priest. This enabled her to celebrate communion in Scotland but has meant that when she returned to her home at Oxford she reverted to being a deacon with no power to celebrate, even though in 1990 she was elected to the General Synod. It seems both inevitable and desirable that these absurdities should soon come to an end.

On becoming an ambassador, as the Queen's representative, one almost inevitably takes on an official relationship with the established church and its offshoots, although I thought it regrettable that some of my colleagues found it necessary to advertise their unbelief by ostentatiously distancing themselves from Anglican representatives. In Israel however my relations with the Anglican set-up were more personal than official. In Tel Aviv itself we had a tiny congregation, consisting mostly of members of the Embassy, one or two other expatriates and the odd English-speaking tourist. The main manifestation of Anglicanism, inherited from the British Mandate, was St George's Cathedral in Jerusalem. But as it lay in the administered territories rather than in Israel proper, it was the preserve of the Consul-General at Jerusalem, and the Ambassador at Tel Aviv was only allowed there unofficially and on sufferance. The cathedral dignitaries and their flock, though personally very courteous, were bitterly anti-Israeli. Luckily, the only exception was the Archbishop in Jerusalem himself. George Appleton, who saw it as his Christian function not to defend the property rights of his church but to help promote peace in the region. In this he was indefatigable, much to the horror of most of his clergy, and we did our best to support him by helping him to meet prominent Israelis. But it was an uphill struggle.

In Israel proper there was a flourishing Anglican church at Nazareth. As with most Christian communities in the area, its congregation was exclusively Arab. It celebrated its centenary while we were there. Robert Stopford, then Bishop of London and formerly of Fulham and Delos, came out to preach the sermon. I had to read the lesson. His words and mine constituted the only English spoken during the proceedings. The service paper was written in English starting from the front and in Arabic starting from the back. We sang the hymns each in his own language but to the same tune. It must have been quite a feat to fit the Arabic language into the metrical straitjacket of *Hymns Ancient & Modern*.

One of our visitors in Israel was Robin Woods, a very old friend, brother-in-law of Budge Firth, former chaplain of Trinity, then Bishop of Worcester, married to Henrietta, with whom I had been to kindergarten in Birmingham. As he had been Dean of St George's, Windsor, we thought fit to take him to the tomb of St George at Lod, otherwise Lydda. When we announced ourselves, the Archimandrite bade us join him in his quarters. As it was Easter Monday, the entertainment consisted of us all taking coloured hard-boiled eggs and bashing them against each other, as if playing conkers. Never did I expect to see a bishop of the established Church and a Greek orthodox priest banging their eggs together while shouting 'Christos aneste' (Christ is risen) when the other man's egg disintegrated.

In Holland we found ourselves much closer to the Anglican establishment again. Once more we were in the diocese of Fulham but now the Bishop was John Satterthwaite, whom I had known for years as the Foreign Secretary of the Church of England who kept in close touch with Foreign Office officials. During that time he had invited me to a dining club which he ran at the Athenaeum, with discussions with some special guest after dinner. Two occasions stick in my memory. Once the guest of honour was John Betjeman and I had hoped to hear him discourse on the architecture of English parish churches or some such subject. Not a bit of it. He sat there telling us of the tribulations in the Betjeman household, with his wife a Catholic and himself a Protestant, tears pouring down his face all the time. All very sad and very embarrassing. The other time was when Mervyn Stockwood, Bishop of Southwark, came to talk about his 'theological college without walls'. He ran it with John Robinson, then Suffragan Bishop of Woolwich, and the idea was to have evening classes to train for the priesthood men who were already engaged in secular professions. When we were asked for our comments, I most unwisely, given the nature of the audience, suggested that, if people were going to do two jobs at once, one lay and one spiritual, there must be several professions for which it would be valuable to ordain women. From the moment I opened my mouth, it was clear that I had put my foot in it. Stockwood looked at me pityingly and said 'I shall not enter into the theological arguments on this. But on the practical level, if you put a woman in charge of a church, you are liable to arrive one day and find a notice saying "This church closed for nine months".' I did not think this a very episcopal or even spiritual argument and, when I told the tale to a girl friend, she said 'But surely a surplice would cover up all that anyway.'

The Bishop of Fulham, who was also titular Bishop of Gibraltar, had a tricky assignment in that he had to administer a diocese to which most of the incumbents were appointed by the Commonwealth and Continental Church Society, familiarly known as the Com and Con. The Society's traditions were on the evangelical side of things whereas the diocesan authorities leaned more towards the High Church persuasion. But John Satterthwaite's diplomatic skills were fully equal to this challenge and he was greatly assisted by the financial acumen of his assistant bishop, Harold Isherwood. On one occasion when John Satterthwaite was staying with us, another guest was our old friend Hugh Springer, later to be Governor-General of Barbados. We thought it fitting to have a white bishop and a black knight in the house together. Checkmate.

There were the best part of a dozen Anglican chaplaincies distributed over the Netherlands. I was naturally most closely involved in The Hague chaplaincy as we lived in the town. Like Gaul, the congregation was divided into three parts: British, North American and Dutch. The British and Americans were mostly expatriates, many of them working for companies like Shell. The Dutch, often descendants of mixed marriages, mostly spoke their own language during the week and worshipped in English on Sundays. This tripartite division inevitably led to some tensions. There was also trouble because a group in the church had become 'charismatic' and antagonised the rest of the congregation. This was my first experience of charismatics, but luckily it had not taken an extreme form. As far as I know, there was no 'speaking with tongues' in what its opponents called jabberwocky language. But the divisions were sharp enough and the fur flying fast enough for the Bishop of London, Gerald Ellison, to come and have a look at the situation. As he said, it was difficult to fault a parish where the church was full every Sunday and the finances were flourishing. But his visitation, combined with some personal changes, almost certainly had an eirenic effect.

We went fairly regularly to other Anglican churches, notably at Amsterdam and the Missions to Seamen at Rotterdam, where there were flourishing congregations. Very occasionally one had to give an address which should not be called a sermon, but usually one could get away with reading a lesson.

The Church of Scotland was represented by a delightful smallish church in the Begijnhof at Amsterdam. It had been there since 1400 and some of the Pilgrim fathers had worshipped there before setting sail for New England. We usually sat under the monument to Daniel Brewster, which made us feel at home, as in 1961/62 we had lived in his Brewster Street in Cambridge, Massachusetts and also because he had come from the little village of Scrooby in Lincolnshire, where our eldest daughter was then just starting married life. The church was under repair when we arrived in Holland but when restoration was complete Queen Elizabeth, the Queen Mother, agreed to come out for the reopening. Her Majesty was kind enough to stay with us and no one could have asked for a more gracious or delightful guest. We naturally gave up our bedroom, as the best room in the house, to the Queen

Mother. At about 2 a.m. I woke up to the realisation that I had never warned Her Majesty that the bell push beside her bed, which she might wish to use to summon her maid, was in fact a security button connected to the police station, so that a posse of officers might suddenly appear in the royal bedroom. Luckily it did not happen.

But we were not confined to the Anglican or even British fold. The Dutch are a nation of merchants and parsons and their religious interests are as highly developed as their commercial skills. It is said that even the Catholics in Holland are Calvinists. But the historical divisions still persist. Traditionally the south, below the Rivers Rhine and Maas, was Catholic and the north Protestant, although the distinction is no longer so clear cut. The religious divide persists in many aspects of the national life. In politics, there is a strong Catholic party, two prominent Protestant parties and a solid Socialist party, although in a country which practises full proportional representation there is a myriad of smaller and often ephemeral parties as well. It used to be said that if three Germans met together they would form a federation, whereas three Dutchmen would comprise one party and two splinter groups. In Holland there were, under the principle of Verzuiling, or pillarisation, a Catholic trade union, a Protestant trade union and a secular trade union. There were also Catholic, Protestant and Socialist broadcasting organisations. The political divisions were vertical rather than horizontal.

Nor was this all. Holland was the home of the old Catholic Church, with whom the Anglican Church is in communion and we had frequent and happy contacts with Archbishop Kok of Utrecht. There were indeed two Archbishops of Utrecht, one Old Catholic and one Roman Catholic, a situation similar to that of Armagh in Northern Ireland. When we arrived, the Roman Catholic Archbishop of Utrecht was Cardinal Alfrink, a parish priest writ large and an intensely modest man. He wore no scarlet trimmings and one could easily mistake him for one of the lesser clergy, as I once did to my shame at a cocktail party in our own house, just realising my mistake in time. He certainly did not expect the attentions often required by cardinals, such as being escorted to the door with lighted candelabra above their heads. I once saw Prince Schwarzenberg struggling to see out two cardinals at one time from the Austrian Embassy in Belgrave Square. As they emerged into the London climate, needless to say the candles promptly went out, leaving the unfortunate Ambassador vainly attempting to revive them with a lighted match at full arm's length.

Alfrink's successor was Cardinal Willibrands, who came to Utrecht from the Secretariat for Christian Unity, founded by Cardinal Bea, at the Vatican and was to return there after quite a short time. I called on him once and had the impression that he was more interested in international diplomacy than in the internal administration of the Church in the Netherlands. But this may well just have been his good manners in conversation with an ambassador. The Church certainly had its internal problems. Many of its nominal adherents were Christians who did not go to church. Priests were leaving to be married. Few were coming forward for ordination. There was pressure for the ordination of women. The bench of bishops was split between the liberals who wanted to accommodate to these trends and the conservatives demanding a reimposition of discipline. After our time things had reached such a pass that the Pope summoned all the Dutch bishops to Rome, knocked their heads together and made them toe the conservative line, which he reinforced by several new appointments.

One of the liberals was a special friend, Bishop Zwartkruis of Haarlem. He had a cottage in Ireland and a keen and informed interest in English literature. He was delighted, for example, when we asked him to luncheon to meet Margaret Drabble. His special pride and joy at Haarlem was a fourteenth century gilt crozier, of Lower Rhineland workmanship, of which the only other comparable example is in the V & A. He asked us to luncheon to see it. After a delicious meal served by nuns, he led us into his bedroom and drew the crozier out from its hiding place under the bed. We need not have bothered about the nonagenarian Maronite patriarch all those years earlier.

Strangely enough, our own house at The Hague belonged to the Roman Catholic Church. In the eighteenth century the house had been rebuilt by a Spanish ambassador, who being a devout Catholic had built himself a private chapel as well. As for 300 years only Dutch Reformed Churches could show their face in public, the chapel had been built behind the house. The Spaniard then left the whole complex to the Jesuits. It was from the Jesuits that the British Government later rented the property. But, although they were prepared to rent a house for their servants to occupy, they jibbed at renting a Catholic chapel too. It was ironic that when we paid rent for the house, it was conveyed to Father Brenninkmeijer, SJ, of the family which owned C & A Stores.

I did not think that his need was greater than ours. Meanwhile the chapel reverted to being a regular Catholic church, but, as it was behind the house and served by the same entrance, we had to leave the main gate open by day to enable the faithful to attend mass. This had the tragic consequence that when my poor successor, Richard Sykes, was murdered at the front door, the assassins had been able to hide in the church porch and emerge from there to shoot him.

One perk of my time in Holland was an invitation to fly in Concorde, on a proving flight before it went into commercial service. We only flew as far as Spain and back without landing, but this enabled us to go supersonic. We had an all-star cast, including George Reindorp, then Bishop of Salisbury. When we reached an altitude of 54,000 feet, he rubbed his hands together with glee and said 'This is splendid; no bishop has ever been so close to heaven before.' At that point the air hostess came up and asked if he would like another drink. 'No, my dear,' pointing upwards, 'we are much too close to headquarters.'

I suppose it was inevitable that after retirement I should become further embroiled in Church affairs. At first I concentrated on writing my father's life, which should have been done a quarter of a century earlier, when the events and the controversies were still topical. Nor did it help that my publishers, Collins, lost £1 million that year, so that they felt obliged nearly to double the selling price for which we had signed a contract. Not many people would have bought the book even at £7.95; still fewer wanted it at £12.95. But soon I was telling people that I was doing odd jobs in the City of London, the County of Sussex and the Church of England.

The first Church job was to join a committee to form a Diocese in Europe to replace the titular diocese of Fulham and Gibraltar. The new diocese was to embrace all the previous chaplaincies on the Continent, but was to be an integral part of the Church of England, with representation in the General Synod and other delights. We had both to prepare a measure to be passed by the General Synod and then presented to Parliament for approval and also to draft the constitution for the diocese itself. It fell largely to my lot to draft the constitution, with the invaluable cooperation of Brian Hanson, legal adviser to the General Synod and a neighbour of ours in Sussex. One of our problems was the title of the new diocese. Fulham was out as it would no longer be under the suzerainty of the Bishop of London. Gibraltar seemed to us out in another sense, out on a limb at the edge of the Continent.

There was a pro-cathedral at Valletta but the diocese of Malta sounded altogether too colonialist in the age of Mintoff. Other territorial titles would be arbitrary and could be awkward. What would the Pope have said to another Bishop of Rome? Even Bishop in Europe struck us as arrogant when there were other Protestants within the European Community. So we settled for Bishop in Europe, much as there used to be a Grand Duke of Bavaria and a Duke in Bavaria. So it was enshrined in the constitution. But unluckily the bishop later found that for certain legal purposes he had to retain the Gibraltar connexion and took to calling himself Bishop of Gibraltar in Europe, which I personally regard as the worst of all worlds, as well as the negation of my handiwork.

It was again perhaps inevitable that I should be asked to join the council of the new diocese. But it brought me into touch with some pleasant people and we met in some pleasant places, including a particularly delightful villa outside Milan. I stayed on the Council until the statutory time for the revision of the constitution after the necessary period of trial and error. My paternity of the original version entitled me to defend my offspring against too much mutilation. Then I felt it time to resign so that I could be replaced by someone with more up-to-date knowledge of the diocesan area.

For by this time most of my travels abroad, except for holidays, were to Israel, where the Rothschild family had generously invited me to join the Council of the Open University. It had originally been called Everyman's University, but this displeased the feminists and those who wanted to raise funds from every woman too. By now I was also a member of the British Trust for the Institute of Oecumenical Studies at Tantur, between Jerusalem and Bethlehem. The chairman of the Trust to begin with was Robin Woods, of Easter-egg fame at St George's tomb at Lydda. Then George Carey of Bath and Wells took over and very impressive he was. Nothing could have given me greater pleasure than George's appointment to Canterbury. He has a fine brain, a most attractive personality and a real power of leadership. I had said to many people that he ought to be chosen but never dared to hope that the powers that be would be so sensible. So in Israel I was able to combine my university and oecumenical duties on the same visits. As I was also a member of Teddy Kollek's Jerusalem Committee, the various functions dovetailed in quite well together. Kollek, the famous Mayor of Jerusalem, had created this international committee to help him resist attempts by the Government of Israel or other misguided well-wishers to ruin the amenities of the Holy City. Many of its members were town planners of alarming technical virtuosity. But some of us were generalists, such as Ursula Niebuhr, widow of Reinhold, whose lectures we had attended at Harvard in 1961/62. Ursula was the first woman to gain a first in theology at Oxford. She has also known everybody who was anybody in the Church of England for the past fifty years and, as she has total recall, would have been far better equipped than I am to write these reminiscences of the period and people with which I am concerned. I hope and believe that she has been doing so.

So much for the international side of things, except that the Nikaean Club also had an international dimension, having been founded as a link with the Eastern Churches and spending much of its time entertaining oriental dignitaries with elaborate pectoral crosses. But for me it offered an opportunity to meet kindred spirits and, very occasionally, to have some informal contact with the Archbishop of Canterbury. Whatever may be thought or said, by people like Dr Gary Bennett, about his public and official persona, in private Dr Runcie has a relaxed and totally unpompous charm and in after-dinner speeches a delicious sense of humour. No doubt he enjoyed being the centre of the picture and perhaps he did not give strong leadership to the Church; but when celebrating communion for the Nikaean Club in a plain off-white cassock in the crypt chapel of Lambeth Palace, he showed a simple and impressive humility. But he can handle elaborate ceremonial too. He participated at a requiem mass at St Alban's, Holborn, for my friend Cheslyn Jones, who had been at the Dragon and Winchester with me, had become Principal of Chichester Theological College and of Pusey House at Oxford and had grown more and more eccentric with the years. Richard Eyre, Dean of Exeter, preached a most amusing and affectionate sermon at the requiem, asking what Cheslyn himself would have said about the occasion. 'Hm, hm, Archbishop too; well, well, you never can tell.'

Cheslyn was a dear friend throughout our lives. When we were newly married, he was a Benedictine monk at Nashdom Abbey and often came to spend the weekend with us. Whisky was then in short supply and it was nothing for Cheslyn to down a month's ration during the weekend. We did not begrudge it to him but were not surprised that he did not last long as a monk. When he was Principal at Chichester, we received an invitation to celebrate the 25th anniversary of his ordination at 12 noon one day. We arrived on the dot with our tongues hanging out, expecting champagne, only to find that it was a celebration of a different kind and we just squeezed into the chapel in time, incidentally for a wonderful piece of liturgical invention, the Magnificat sung to a ukelele and all. He was a fine scholar but never fulfilled his early promise, failing, for example, to publish anything, not even his Bampton Lectures. But he did agree, in 1964, somewhat reluctantly as he thought we were bypassing the parish church, to christen our youngest son in our drawing-room.

Runcie's predecessor, Donald Coggan, has been a good friend, for whom I have the greatest admiration. I first met him when he visited Israel as Archbishop of York. Speaking after dinner in Jerusalem, he told how Winston Churchill had said that there were only two things harder than making an after-dinner speech: climbing a wall leaning towards you and kissing a girl leaning away from you. Since then, whenever I have stolen that story myself, I have been able to claim that it must be respectable, having been told to me by an archbishop.

In the Chichester diocese, my most lasting job was to be chairman for over ten years of the Redundant Churches Uses Committee. When a church is declared redundant, three courses are open: to find an alternative use for it, to put it into mothballs under the Redundant Churches Fund or to demolish it. Our committee's main task was to find an alternative use. I always thought it the last refuge of the destitute, and a confession of failure, to have recourse to the Fund, which depended on public money and not too much of that. Demolition usually aroused agonised reproaches, though mostly from people who had no money to put where their mouth was. So we had to exercise our ingenuity to find alternative uses. One of our first achievements was to sell a church in Hove to Brighton and Hove Albion Football Club, which was then in the Second Division. I wanted to wait until it reached the First Division, when we could have held out for a higher price. But the committee were in a hurry to dispose of the church and were ready to sell. Needless to say, a year or two later Brighton duly reached the First Division. But as they soon dropped out of it again, our losses were probably not too serious.

We leased another church to Brighton Corporation for conversion into a Museum of Brighton under the auspices of the Royal Pavilion. As I was also a trustee of the friends of the Pavilion, the chairman of the

Diocesan Board of Finance not surprisingly seemed doubtful for which side I was batting and it took a bit of time and effort to convince him that of course I had the interests of the diocese absolutely at heart.

The Bishop of Chichester, Eric Kemp, thought it would be useful for me and my redundant churches if I met more people in the diocese and he kindly co-opted me as a member of his Diocesan Synod. It was certainly an excellent opportunity to make friends, even if my contributions to debates on subjects ranging from nuclear weapons to surrogate motherhood rarely seemed to meet with approval from a body which combined conservative attitudes on religious matters with surprisingly left-wing political views. But this was a phenomenon which I had noted in earlier days: the Anglo-Catholic clergy toiled away in the slums whereas my father's Modernist friends, for example Dean Inge, hobnobbing with Beaverbrook, were mostly high Tories. Only a handful, such as Charles Raven and Dick Sheppard, were liberal in both doctrine and politics.

Of the two suffragan bishops in the Chichester diocese, Colin Docker, then Bishop of Horsham, had been confirmed by my father and, when he came to conduct a confirmation in our village church, claimed that this must have something to do with the apostolic succession. As chairman of the Diocesan Board for Social Responsibility he was also immensely helpful to me in my capacity as chairman of the Sussex Rural Community Council. He incidentally had a voice which would have carried across the Atlantic without the intervention of a telephone.

His brother of Lewes, Peter Ball (now of Gloucester), on the other hand, was almost totally inaudible at anything over a range of three feet. But even so, he was excellent company, even if I did not agree with all his views. As a monk he imposed strict discipline on himself. Once when I had to speak at Hastings on nuclear defence, he was supposed to take the chair. But a message came to say that he had as usual slept on the hard floor and that morning had been unable to get up. That seemed to me to be carrying mortification of the flesh rather far.

The Dean of Chichester, Robert Holtby, enlisted me to take the chair of the committee to raise funds for restoration of the cathedral organ. This instrument designed by Renatus Harris was some three hundred years old and one of the two oldest cathedral organs in England. But it had started to emit unfortunate noises at inappropriate moments and had had to be put out of commission and temporarily replaced by an electronic organ atop the choir screen. The cost of restoration was to be over £250,000 and there were not lacking people to say that it was wicked to spend so much money on a musical instrument when the church was in great need both for the ministry and the laity. But, largely by dint of appealing to people who were interested in music and would not have subscribed to other causes, we raised the money without too much difficulty and were able to ask Ted Heath to speak at the service to inaugurate the new organ.

The dean also once asked me to preach in the Cathedral. But afterwards his only comment was that he was glad the bishop had not been there to hear some of my heretical remarks. I admit that I had trailed my coat. I was not asked again.

So I have wound my way down the backstairs, meeting many people who were on their way up, although most of those whom I have mentioned here would have been going up the front stairs anyway. I can only in my very small way emulate Louis XIV, of whom it was said that, when he met a chambermaid on the stairs, he stood aside to let her pass.

2
A Tale of Four Universities

Most people spend three years or so of their youth at a university and, unless becoming dons, leave the groves of Academe for ever. This was not to be my fate.

For my parents too it was different. My father had spent twenty years as Fellow, Dean and tutor of Trinity, Cambridge, before he married and went to London, as Master of the Temple. When my mother was born, in 1881, her father was Vice-Chancellor at Manchester, which our daughter Mel was to attend a century later. In her 'teens he became Master of Peterhouse, Cambridge. She herself had read English at Royal Holloway College and, being born before the age of radio and television, belonged to a well-read generation. For both of them, the university, or perhaps what Newman called 'the Idea of a University', was their spiritual home. They judged people by university standards. 'What degree did he get?' was the usual first question about any new acquaintance.

It never occurred to me that I should not go to Cambridge, nor for that matter to Trinity. In those days there were none of the agonies of A-levels and UCCA forms. One took a scholarship examination largely because Winchester expected it. The scholarship was means-tested and worth very little money. The only advantage was that one could spend all three undergraduate years in rooms in college, instead of having to find 'digs' for two of them.

On the subject of digging, Cambridge in the 1930s is now generally regarded as the burrowing ground of Communist moles. It did not seem so at the time. True, in the age of the dictators, we were all inclined to lean to the left. Indeed, there was even a Communist President of the Union in my time, and he was Michael Whitney Straight, the American millionaire who later 'blew' Blunt. He also invited the exiled Emperor of Abyssinia to become an honorary member of the Union. Haile Selassie duly turned up, in bowler hat and blue cloak, to receive this great honour. Aubrey Eban was to tell me later that, as Secretary of the Union around this time, he had to correspond with the Emperor and the reply came back headed 'His Imperial Majesty Haile Selassie the First, Emperor of Ethiopia, by Divine Protection, Divider of the Oceans from the Lands, Lion of Judah, King of Kings . . . 22 Smith Street, Bath'. Thus were the mighty fallen. But he did get his throne back, for a time.

Most of us were more vaguely opponents of fascism. There was only one known member of the Cambridge University Fascist Club. Coming late to a party at Trinity, consisting mainly of members of the Vic-Wells Ballet, he screwed his monocle into his eye and observed 'Before leaving one will obviously have to take a roll or two on the floor.' Or so it was said. He later became a general.

Most of us joined the Left Book Club and subscribed to Claud Cockburn's *The Week*, the latter a spicy concoction of Marxist propaganda and Mayfair gossip. The Spanish Civil War was at its height. Every evening the newsboy under my window kept shouting 'Terrible scenes in Madrid' and every week at the Union names were read out of members who had been speaking there the term before but had since been killed in Spain.

I once even volunteered to canvass for the Labour Party in a local election. But when I rang a bell and found myself confronted on the doorstep by my grandmother's former parlourmaid, my courage deserted me and to my shame I could not face urging her to vote Labour.

But it was not all politics. Some of the older dons had been fellows with my father and were generous in entertaining me. They were a distinguished lot. It used to be said that, if the wall behind the High Table had collapsed during dinner in hall, half the members of the Order of Merit would have perished at a stroke. Many stories were told of the absent-mindedness of the Master, J. J. Thomson, OM, who looked the typical vague professor, and at first sight he seemed a formidable figure, having split the atom, but he soon put one at one's ease by knowing the college cricket averages by heart. My father said that he also knew all the episcopal appointments before they were announced.

Winstanley, the Vice-Master, had a nice wit. He used to compare Drake, finishing his bowls on Plymouth Hoe as the Armada approached the Channel, with Charles II continuing to chase butterflies at Whitehall while the Dutch were sailing up the Medway: both finished their fun first, but the essential difference was that Drake won and Charles lost. History backs the winners.

My father was sorry, as I was, that he could not introduce me to A. E. Housman, who died the year before I went up. It is hard to remember how fashionable Housman was as a poet in the late 1930s. When he walked across from Whewell's Court to dine in hall, people would gather in Trinity Street to touch the hem of his gown.

F. A. Simpson, another of my father's friends, was notorious for cutting the ivy in Great Court with his nail-scissors. He was still doing so when our elder son went up thirty years later. He had once written a book on the Second Empire but, dissatisfied with its reception, never put pen to paper again. Similarly, he had one sermon which he was willing to deliver if every other detail of the service was just as he ordered. The day came when the wrong psalm was sung. Simpson insisted on an apology. The apology was not abject enough. He asked for greater grovelling. This was refused and he never preached that sermon again. An amusing memoir of him, entitled *A Last Eccentric* was published in 1991.

Another distinguished eccentric, the University Registrary, Harrison, was reputed to write Greek verse better than Euripides and almost as well as Sophocles. When the second war came, he was, with the head porter and chef, appointed a college air-raid warden. They were set an examination paper on their duties. The head porter got 100%, the chef over 90%, but Harrison, to the general astonishment, only 75%. This needed some investigation. It was found that one question had been 'What is your first action on smelling gas?' The right answer is 'Hold your breath'. Harrison with scholarly precision thought this could not be right, as holding your breath is not an action but a suspension of action.

Wittgenstein to my regret I never met, although I believe that he was in residence when I was up. He was alleged to furnish his rooms with a deck-chair and two soap-boxes and it was said of him that he thought so intensely that every five minutes he had to make his mind a blank, otherwise his brain would have seized up.

My first tutor was Jim Butler, whose father had been Master and who had lived almost all his days at Trinity. His mother had been a Christian Scientist; when her children were evidently infectious, she had alarmed other Cambridge parents, of whom my grandmother was one, by sending them to parties and asserting there was nothing wrong with them. There were those who said that if Jim's brother Nevile had not been Lothian's No. 2 at the Washington Embassy in 1940, Lothian, a Christian Scientist himself, might have been persuaded to be medically treated and might not have died there then.

Jim Butler lived in my father's old rooms. When my father had them he used to leave the brochures of his insurance company in his pupils' waiting-room. On the strength of this advertisement, he became an agent of the company. I succeeded him in this and to this day deduct 15% from all my premiums.

Left-wing or not, we did ourselves quite well and sometimes took ourselves too seriously. One of the pleasures of Trinity, for example, was the Vatel Club, named after Louis XIV's chef, where undergraduate posed pompously as connoisseurs of food and drink. After dinner each of us had to rise and give his verdict. One member, later a Cabinet Minister, could only blurt out 'Ze fisch wazh frightful' and sit down. Another spoke learnedly on whether Dubonnet or Du Bonnet was or were one or two words. Once we invited the senior partner of Berry's of St James's to join us. He accepted on condition that he supplied the wines; we demurred politely but not for too long. When the evening came, one glance at the menu, which I still have, suggested that one would be carried out feet foremost after the fish; but Mr Berry had planned the counterpoint of food and wine so well that we went through nine courses and twelve drinks without turning a hair. We started with that rarity, a vintage sherry, in this case 1888, and ended with a brandy of 1848, year of revolutions. On another occasion, dinner was supplied by an Alsatian, a native of Alsace, not a dog. The dining-room was rather far from the kitchen, so that when the cheese fondu arrived, most of us plunged our forks into it and found ourselves tugging at Excalibur; others, less lucky, had been able to convey some to their mouths, gravely endangering their teeth.

No doubt this was all shockingly frivolous and extravagant. But less so than it seems now. Those were the days when you could have a shave for 1d (one old penny) and a close shave for 2d.

We had to do some work too, in my case the Classical Tripos. The first two years of Part I were pretty dreary, serving up weekly Latin and Greek prose and verse compositions, much as one had done for the last two years at school. For the so-called University Scholarships, one had to compose a free Latin ode on one of several set subjects. As this had to be done within three hours, I was advised to write it in advance and learn it by heart. This being early in 1939, I assumed that one subject would be concerned with Chamberlain and Munich. So I duly prepared and memorised several stanzas on that theme. But to my horror, I found no such subject on the paper. Luckily however one of the choices was the 1938 State Visit of the King and Queen to Canada and the USA. It took me two laborious hours to put together an opening stanza to our monarchs 'who had travelled across the seas to bring peace to the peoples, just like Mr Chamberlain ('Cancellarius iste') who . . . ' and so on with my prefabricated verse and a huge sigh of relief.

One of my friends was less lucky. Looking down the subjects for this free Latin verse, he saw the name of Micius Mus and assumed this was a distinguished Roman consul. Only too late did he recognise Mickey Mouse.

For Park II of the Tripos I chose to specialise in ancient history. Trinity, having no ancient historians, suggested that I should supervise myself. This seemed the straight road to failure; so I insisted on instruction and was sent to Guy Griffith at Caius College next door. He had written vast tracts of the *Cambridge Ancient History*, but also, with Michael Oakeshott, a little yellow-covered book on *How to Spot the Classic Winners*, in another sense of the Classics. When I went to read my essay, he served sherry in huge opaque blue beakers, so that one could not see how much was in them. The conversation went like this: 'Wonderful athletes the Greeks. Must have been great horsemen. How would they compare with today's riders? Who's going to win the Derby?' By then so much sherry had been drunk that I could hardly see to read my essay. Nor did the other advice help much: Griffith was all for backing a Hyperion colt that year, but Blue Peter won in a canter.

I found it easiest to cram preparation for the examinations into intensive work in the last fortnight. Imagine my chagrin when, just as I was starting this late sprint, came a letter from my father: 'now is the time to relax and ensure that you are in good fettle for the examination.' Anyhow I duly took my degree. Not that this classical learning helped much. The war started three months later and when it ended I could not have translated a page of Caesar or an inscription on a tombstone.

So much for undergraduate days. My next encounter with a university came a quarter of a century later, when in 1961 I was sent on a sabbatical year to Harvard, masquerading as a Fellow of the Center for

International Affairs. The Fellows each year consisted of two representatives from the State Department, one from each of the American armed services and one diplomat or official from each of about a dozen other countries. We were supposed to 'broaden our background and deepen our insight'. It was certainly rewarding to be able to talk freely with one's colleagues from other diplomatic services, knowing that we were all expressing our own opinions and not just repeating our governments' instructions.

Much of our time was spent in seminars, usually guided by a member of the Harvard faculty, including a then almost unknown professor called Henry Kissinger. These were the early days of the Kennedy era, when academic advisers were commuting between Cambridge, Massachusetts, and Washington. Indeed it was said that the United States was governed at that time by Harvard professors and Oxford Rhodes Scholars. Even then Kissinger was outstanding among them. Most people in the strategic business in those days saw the world as bipolar, consisting only of Washington and Moscow. But Kissinger was already insisting that it was polycentric, that the United States needed allies, had allies and should take account of her allies. Even so, years later he was to advise Nixon to visit China without consulting the Japanese and to devalue the dollar without warning Germany.

Those were the heady days of strategic game-theory, with professors calculating that warfare was or was not a zero-sum game and arguing that if the Russians 'took out' Chicago, the Americans must at once take out Kiev. It all sounded very tidy on the chessboard and in those days a nuclear war certainly seemed possible, indeed even probable, whether or not it could be so easily controlled. But from the time of Cuba 1962, when the Russians under Kruschev made clear that they were not going to challenge the United States to nuclear combat, it has seemed far less likely, if not outright unthinkable. Cuba was the watershed of nuclear confrontation. This was also the lesson of Checkpoint Charlie, of Czechoslovakia 1968 and indeed of Vietnam. In the last resort the Soviet Union would not risk nuclear war. So the nuclear deterrent had to be maintained and the right to first use of it also had to be retained. But there is a world of difference between first use and first strike. Hence the abandonment of the light-hearted theories of those early game-strategists; the rejection of the concepts of massive retaliation and mutual assured destruction, suitably known as MAD, the study of interforce rather than intercity strategies; the realisation that, once the firebreak between conventional and nuclear has been passed, escalation is all too difficult to control; and the adoption of the doctrine of flexible response, while the Cold War lasted.

Apart from discussions on these high matters in seminars, one was only required to produce one paper and conduct a debate on it. I used the chance to study the political and economic structure of Yugoslavia, as an object lesson in 'market communism' or 'communism with a human face', in order to suggest that, if we could stomach a national variety of communism in Yugoslavia, independent of the Soviet bloc, we might be able to tolerate or even encourage a similar unorthodoxy in Cuba or even in China. But at that date such ideas evoked no echoes in American breasts.

Altogether it was a stimulating year, enabling one to recharge one's batteries, even though my colleague from the US Air Force lamented to me after four weeks there that he had been at the Center for International Affairs for a month, but had not even had a domestic affair yet. We were allowed to attend any lectures at the university we liked. I could have taken a cookery course, had I wanted. My wife and I went three mornings a week to hear Reinhold Niebuhr, in a course called 'The Open and Closed Society', dissect the morning's headlines and distil wisdom from them. My wife also sat at the feet of Paul Tillich and one day dragged me to hear him speak on Marx and Nietzsche as existentialists; I listened spellbound for an hour and only when I came out realised that I had not understood a single word.

We made some good friends at Harvard. Hugh Springer, later Governor-General of Barbados, was often to be our guest in England and The Hague. Jörg Kastl, who became German Ambassador at Moscow, once took me to call on Heinrich Bruening, the former Chancellor of the Weimar Republic, at Dartmouth, Vermont. It was a depressing visit. Bruening clearly thought that he ought to have been recalled as Chancellor when the new Federal Republic was formed and passed his time in solitary seclusion in a Nissen hut, inveighing bitterly against Konrad Adenauer, whom he accused of deliberately supplanting him. He was a bad loser, but Adenauer had probably never even seen it as a contest.

My Japanese colleague, Hiro Uchida, later Ambassador at The Hague, but alas, not in our time, came to Bosham in Sussex the year after we all left Harvard. We went to see him and his lovely wife,

Emiko, there and found him faultlessly dressed in yachting cap, blazer and white ducks, but half the size of all the other yachtsmen striding around similarly attired. They once entertained us all to dinner at Harvard. Since their dining-room was not big enough for the whole party, dinner was served in two sittings. To decide who went in to the 'premier service' we were made to play spillikins and other Japanese games on the floor. We had assumed that couples would be divided between the sittings. But no: my wife and I both proved very bad at Japanese games, so that with ruthless oriental logic we were relegated to the 'deuxième service'. The same applied to my Greek Cypriot colleague and his wife. When we eventually came to table, with Mrs Cypriot immaculate as ever in black satin and diamonds, we were each confronted with two chopsticks and a bowl, into which our hostess then broke a raw egg. Mrs Cypriot's eyes widened in horror, as she evidently thought that she was going to spend the evening chasing a raw egg round the bottom of her bowl with chopsticks. Her spirits revived when the full delights of sukiyaki were revealed.

As we were without diplomatic status, we had to file a tax return before leaving the country. I went down to do this with my Japanese and Indian colleagues and the tax collector, who was presumably a racist, bade me as a Caucasian explain the tax form to my two colleagues, who were in fact at least as capable of doing so as I was. While we were thus engaged, a perfectly good American citizen approached and with great deference asked me to expound the tax system. I had to explain that I was just another victim of it.

It had all been rather like going back to school. Indeed, when I went to have my hair cut by the university barber, there was a notice saying 'Haircut $1.50; Students $1'. When I demanded a dollar haircut, the barber replied 'A bit older than the other stoodents, aren't you?' In the end he relented, but retaliated by giving me a student crewcut.

We managed to put in a good deal of sightseeing. Once on a visit to the Barnes Collection (no relation) at Philadelphia, we combined this with meeting my wife's cousin, Darlington Hoopes, who had stood as Socialist candidate for President in 1952, Eisenhower's first election year, and had scored 20,000 votes out of 60 million. He was far from being one's image of an American politician. When I tried, as I thought tactfully, to make conversation about socialist doctrine, he soon stopped me. 'Don't worry about that. I'm not a Marxist. I'm a Christian Socialist.' He was in fact a Quaker and a teetotaller. After an evening with him, one of his friends asked us home for a drink. We accepted eagerly. When we arrived, this friend handed each of us a glass and led us through the house to the garden behind, where a spring was gushing from the hillside. 'This', he said, 'is the best water in Pennsylvania.'

Anyhow, we left Harvard much refreshed by the renewed contact with academic life and kept in touch with several friends from those days. Harvard has a vigorous alumni association in London and we have attended some of its gatherings, including an excellent evening at Emmanuel, Cambridge, John Harvard's old college. In the 1980s, too, Jean-Paul van Bellinghem, Belgian Ambassador at London and also a former Fellow of the Center, organised several successful old boys' reunions at his embassy. The vintages of nearly thirty years make quite an interesting bunch.

So when I eventually retired to Sussex in 1977 I thought it would be interesting to make contact with Sussex University and eventually was asked to join the Court and shortly afterwards the Council. Sussex had of course started off with a bang, as the showpiece of the new generation of redbrick universities, 'Balliol by the Sea'. It had then the reputation of having the best history school in the country, after Peterhouse, Cambridge. But when I joined it, it had fallen on less happy days. While maintaining its highly individual system of instruction, with the warp and the woof of major and contextual courses, it had fallen victim to the epidemic of student unrest and the whole place had become highly politicised. The younger members of the faculty were if anything redder than the students themselves. Trade union activity was strong, among both teachers and taught. Communication between lay members of Council, the academic body and the students seemed to be minimal. As a result, the university's reputation and therefore the quality of the intake had declined. I saw this as Chairman of the Governors of Hurstpierpoint College, where parents were markedly reluctant to send their sons on to what they regarded as a disorderly establishment. By the same token, employers were reluctant to take on people who they feared might be disruptive elements; and this difficulty in finding jobs for graduates reacted in its turn on the standard of applicants.

On top of these shortcomings, just as I arrived on the scene, the government, through the University Grants Committee, were imposing fairly drastic financial economies, likely to result in the closure of departments and the loss of teaching posts. This had resulted in a pretty general rush for cover and self-preservation. Those, mostly scientists, who could command lucrative consultancies, were seeking early retirement. Others were looking for new ways of funding their posts and ensuring their tenure. The result was largely to frustrate the object of the economies and thus to preserve a rigid structure which militated against the introduction of new, young blood. The standard of research at Sussex had always been high and this had deservedly won a great many financial rewards from outside. But research is by and large a matter of individual effort and, at a time of financial stringency, those engaged upon it are naturally tempted to look to their own interests rather than those of the institution as a whole. I sometimes had the impression that many of the dons would have much preferred to run the university without any students at all.

But these generalised comments are, I admit, grossly unfair in many cases. There were many dedicated people who devoted themselves wholeheartedly to running the administration and taking part in the elaborate committee structure. But this in itself was a weakness in the organisation. Many of the administrators, however dedicated, had been in the same jobs for many years and had no great incentive to innovation. Nor was innovation easy when all policy proposals tended to be fed upwards through the hierarchy of committees, so that when they arrived at the decision-making level they had reached a stage of petrification which made any change of direction extremely difficult and only encouraged the nit-pickers. The paperwork was massive; brainstorming was minimal.

But it must be said that the wave of politicisation had already begun to recede. This was partly due to some clear-sighted young people, one of whom in particular, Nigel Savage, has become a successful merchant banker, who saw that the purpose of the students' union was not to embrace and propagate loony-left causes indiscriminately, or to organise strikes, demonstrations and sit-ins, or to pour red ink over visiting American diplomats, but to work steadily through negotiation to promote student welfare and conditions of life on the campus. Some of us tried to encourage this trend and, by personal contact with the student leaders, to develop better relations between them and the Governing Body.

Presiding over all this turmoil, and as Disraeli said of Lord Liverpool, he presided rather than ruled, was the Vice-Chancellor,

Denys Wilkinson. He had an interesting background, of which he himself told us. As a nuclear physicist, he had been engaged in the war on the atom bomb project in the United States. At the end of the war, not feeling well, he had gone to the doctors. They asked him if there was anything he had always very much wanted to do, which might take him about three months. He realised that he was being told he had a dose of radiation and had about three months' active life ahead of him. He said that he had always been interested in the migration of birds and was advised to go and study this subject for three months. He told this to a friend, who said that in that case he must consult Victor Rothschild. Why Victor Rothschild? 'Because the mathematics of bird-migration are the same as those of his subject, which is the movement of spermatozoa in the womb, partly random and partly purposive.' Suffice it to say that he followed the advice and, thirty years after being given three months to live, was Vice-Chancellor of Sussex University.

Wilkinson was flanked by a number of people with whom I found it hard to establish much rapport or make much headway. Even the old diplomatic maxim 'Feed the beast' did not produce much result. I spent four years or more on the Council, one as vice-chairman, largely spent in raising money to fund the annual meeting of the British Association at Sussex. This meant devoting at least two days a week in term time to the university's affairs, sitting on boards and committees. So eventually I came to the conclusion that this time-consuming exercise was not matched by any commensurate influence on the proceedings and I severed my connection with the place.

Now I am rather sorry that I did so, as the next Vice-Chancellor was an old friend, Leslie Fielding, who worked with me in my Foreign Office department twenty years earlier. Since then he had joined the European Commission, serving as their man in Tokyo and then as Director-General for External Relations in the Brussels headquarters. He is the only man I know who speaks both Persian and Japanese, as well as being a lay reader and an expert ballroom dancer. He touches life at many points and I have the impression that he swiftly brought a breath of fresh air, not to say a wind of change, into Sussex University. Unluckily, his term is almost over.

Three down and one to go. The fourth university with which I have been associated is the Open University of Israel. Soon after I retired and had been generously given a room, a secretary and luncheon rights at

Rothschilds' bank, New Court, Victor and Jacob Rothschild together invited me to join the University Council. It was then called Everyman's University, but this title was later changed to make it easier to raise funds from both every man and every woman in the USA. It was the brainchild of Max Rowe, who ran the Rothschild family foundation for the benefit of charitable activities in Israel, Yad Hanadiv. This means the Foundation of the Benefactor and takes its name from the generosity of Baron Edmond de Rothschild, who had originally financed the ventures of Jewish settlers in Palestine, above all in agriculture, and had incidentally introduced pre-phylloxera vines into the country at the two settlements of Rishon-le-Zion (First into Zion) and Zichron Yaakov (the James Memorial: James or Yaakov being Baron Edmond's name in Hebrew). The Baron and his wife are now buried at Zichron Yaakov, in a lovely garden tomb. His son, James, started life as a French baron and ended it as the English Liberal MP for the Isle of Ely. James's widow, Dorothy, or Dollie as she was universally known, was Chancellor of Everyman's University when I joined it and was one of the most wonderful people I have known. It was an immense pleasure to accompany her, trying to act as *cavaliere servente* on journeys to Israel to attend meetings of the Council, over which she presided, even when over ninety, with unsurpassable dignity and charm.

Yad Hanadiv had begun by supporting educational television in Israel. From that it was a natural step to founding an Open University, an institute of distance learning, which gave some of its instruction by television. This was of course supplemented by written material and by technical equipment. If a student wanted to study chemistry in the kitchen at home, he or she could be supplied with the wherewithal to blow the place up if they liked. For there is no central campus, only study centres scattered over the country. But most of the study is done at home in the student's spare time, with perhaps a fortnight's attendance at a summer school.

When I say at home, this could well mean a barrack-room, or a slit trench, or a hospital ward, or a prison cell. For the Open University is also known as the university of the second chance. Anyone who has missed out on a university course at the normal time can apply. No qualifications are required. It seemed to me that in Israel this had a special significance, and a political spin-off. Admittedly a high proportion of our students were teachers who wanted to better their career prospects by adding a degree to their teacher's diploma. But we also had mothers who had been founding families when they might have been at university, soldiers who had been fighting wars, ne'er-do-wells who had dropped out and, above all, oriental Jews, immigrants from Arab countries who, especially if they were girls, had been deprived of any chance of higher education. Broadly speaking, the uneducated in Israel tended to be hawks, whereas doves were more likely to be found among the ranks of the educated. So one hoped, perhaps unjustifiably, that one was making some small contribution to the peace process.

I briefed myself by visiting our own Open University at Milton Keynes, the prototype of all institutes of distance learning. It has of course been going longer and expanded more widely than its Israeli opposite number. But in Israel we fairly soon reached a plateau of some 12,000 students and began to give degrees, which required six years' work. Although at first the academic staff at the centre had been heavily involved in the preparation of courses, we also were able to begin giving them sabbatical years in which they could pursue their own research and, one hoped, advance their careers and reputations by publishing the results of their work. The English Open University has a vast range of publications to its credit.

Apart from Dollie de Rothschild as Chancellor and Jacob Rothschild as Deputy Chancellor, I was for long the only non-Israeli on the Council, until a representative of the American Friends of the University joined us. It was rather shaming that for our benefit all the proceedings were conducted in English, although this is less of a burden for Israelis than it would be for nationals of many other countries. The members formed a distinguished cross-section of Israeli national life: professors, judges, generals, bankers, lawyers, including, until he became President, Haim Herzog himself.

One of my functions was to act as Vice-President of the American Friends and on one occasion this took me to New York to address a fund-raising dinner. I was flown from London to New York, to Tel Aviv and back to London, put up for three nights at the St Regis Hotel and entertained to various meals, all in order to make a speech strictly limited to thirteen minutes. We did raise about $100,000 but I dread to think how much of that went on my expenses, especially as I lost my voice on arrival and very nearly caused it all to be wasted.

It was difficult otherwise to make much contribution to the

university, except to show that there are English people, not Jewish, who maintain a sympathetic interest in Israel. I was not always entirely in agreement over policy. For example, it seemed to me that the choice of subjects for courses too often were of exclusively Jewish concern and reflected the things which differentiate Jews from other people, whereas in Israel's international situation it is surely important to emphasise those things which unite Jews with the rest of mankind. But this of course only applies to certain fields of study, mostly literary, historical and sociological, and not, for example, to mathematics or scientific subjects. In any case I developed a great respect for the academic standards and intellectual honesty of the university authorities.

There is also an international dimension. Courses are translated into English and Spanish and made available to Jewish communities abroad. Some material, most of a less academic kind, is aimed at Arabic speakers, and two of the first score of graduates were in fact Israeli Arabs. It now seems too that an Open University is being established in Moscow, part of *glasnost* no doubt, and the Israeli university is being invited to help with an appropriate contribution.

I can only hope that my visits to the university were not a total waste of Rothschild money. For me they were a godsend, enabling me to keep in touch with old friends and more importantly with the Israeli political scene as it developed. Perhaps this is part of the process which Harvard called 'broadening one's background and deepening one's insight'. Perhaps there is something similar in Council membership in Sussex and in Israel. But a member of the Council of the Open University of Israel can have little in common with an undergraduate reading classics at Cambridge, beyond a wish always to go on learning a little more, climbing the backstairs.

3
Wasted Wartime

The first half of 1939 was spent getting a degree. After that, with war fairly obviously imminent, it seemed pointless to look assiduously for a job and I kept open the option of going back to Cambridge to do some research.

I was still trying to learn some German and had planned to spend some time at a crammer's called Britons in Bonn, under one Captain Webber, known to the Germans as Hauptmann Weber. But with clouds on the international horizon he had moved his establishment to Putney. One might have learned some German as a Briton in Bonn but the chances of doing so as a Briton in Putney were remote, especially as our instructors were nerve-wracked refugees whom we treated so badly that they must have wondered whether they would not have done better after all under Hitler.

I tried it for a few weeks but then, with an American Wykehamist friend, Ben King, hired a small Peugeot and set off for the south of France. We had reached Clermont-Ferrand when the news of the Molotov-Ribbentrop pact broke. So home we came again, stopping off only in Paris for a last delicious dinner at the Restaurant de la Belle Aurore, now alas defunct.

When war started, the Army said I was too blind. So by a process of nepotism I was found a job in the Communications Department of the Foreign Office. This entailed decyphering telegrams on the night shift from 10 p.m. to 6 a.m. Decyphering was done in pairs. My pair was Terence Rattigan. He had made the then princely sum of £25,000 out of *French Without Tears* and each night he placed a bottle of gin between us. The accuracy of our decyphering declined with the level of gin in the bottle.

Most telegrams seemed to be about sunflower seeds which must have been of great strategic significance. But one from Sir William (not sunflower) Seeds in Moscow started: 'I do not care a [spell a word of four letters]'. This was before four-letter words became common currency. We were agog to decypher further. H—O—O—T 'I do not care a hoot what Stalin said in 1934; what matters is what he says now'.

Soon the Army relented of its blindness or mine; in November 1939 Gunner Barnes reported to Arborfield Training Camp for some three months of square-bashing and the like. The only specific instruction I remember is the quartermaster-sergeant saying in exasperated tones: 'You would lose your balls if they weren't tied up in a little bag.' Then I was posted to the OCTU at Shrivenham and, although I spent some six weeks of the course at home with jaundice, this was put down to the incompetent diagnosis of the medical officer. So I lost no seniority and was duly commissioned on time in June 1940, being sent to the 84th Heavy Anti-Aircraft Regiment, which was deployed in the area now covered by London Airport.

The 84th had been recruited from London Transport and most members still thought of each other as in their pre-war jobs. Once I wanted to promote a bright gunner to be lance-bombardier. 'You can't do that. He's on the back.' I wondered if this had some indecent implication. But it turned out to mean that he was a bus-conductor. Between driver and conductor a great gulf was fixed. One did not promote conductors above drivers.

That summer of 1940, of the Battle of Britain, was one of glorious sunshine. It was hard to realise that the fate of nations was being decided far above our heads in those beautiful blue skies. We had already witnessed the miracle of Dunkirk, which had given us a breathing-space. To this day it is hard to understand why Hitler did not follow it up with an invasion of England, rather than relying on air-power alone. It may be that he was confident that his Luftwaffe would do the trick. It may be that he did not have enough landing-craft. Or he may have already decided to attack Russia and concluded that he could leave England to stew in her own juice and to surrender when he had the whole of mainland Europe from the Atlantic to the Urals in his grasp. He may even have calculated, with the pre-war appeasers in mind, that he could persuade the British to join him in his crusade against Communism. It is true that if we had been as logical as the French we might have concluded that the war was lost and surrender was the only course. But certainly I cannot remember anyone talking in those terms. Thanks no doubt in large part to Winston Churchill, no one doubted that we should win in the end.

For part of the Battle of Britain, I was stationed with my 3.7-inch guns in Windsor Great Park. One Sunday afternoon, slumbering in my tent, I heard a noise like a mighty rushing wind followed by a crash. Seizing my revolver I went out to find a Messerschmidt 109 upside down fifty yards away, with the pilot climbing out apparently unhurt. I do not know which of us was more surprised. But as I had a gun in my hand and he did not, I took him prisoner. That was my closest personal contact with the enemy throughout the whole war.

At one time we shared a gun-site with a mixed battery, whose predictor was operated by Sergeant Mary Churchill. I danced with her then in her khaki battledress but was not to meet her again until she came with her husband, Christopher Soames, then European Commissioner, to stay with us at The Hague.

My brother meanwhile had joined the Friends' Ambulance Unit and spent those months at the London Hospital washing the dead bodies of victims of the blitz. Later he found himself in India, conveying drugs over the hump into China by vehicles which, with petrol in short supply, were reported to run exclusively on gin. As a conscientious objector he saw far more of the nasty side of war than I ever did as an army officer.

Towards the end of 1940 I was sent on a junior staff course, where one of my fellow-students was Basil Spence, Camouflage Officer, later to become architect of Coventry Cathedral and member of the Order of Merit. That course led to my appointment to a brigade headquarters at Holyport, near Maidenhead. Some forty years later I went back to the same house, when Christie's were selling its contents. They told us that the day before they had found an unexploded bomb in the roof. We had probably slept under it all unwittingly for months in 1941.

I cannot remember much about my duties at brigade. Among other things, we had to compile a monthly return of messing by-products, to show how much we had saved for the war effort. Late one night, having completed this vital document, I found that I had added pounds avoirdupois of dripping to cubic centimetres of tea-leaves. I was too bored to change it and shortly afterwards we received a special commendation from the GOC London District for a remarkable achievement in effecting savings.

This did not seem to damage my prospects and after a few months I was promoted captain, as GSo3, 1st Anti-Aircraft Division in Knightsbridge. We were responsible for the whole anti-aircraft defence of the London area, although by now, mid-1941, the worst of the blitz was over. So for six months I had a pretty easy life in the middle of London, covering roughly the period from Operation Barbarossa to Pearl Harbour.

Our amenities in the division were provided by Cecily Courtneidge's Ack-Ack Comforts Fund. One night, by way of thank-you, we entertained the whole cast of her current show to dinner at Grosvenor House. Our general, a former Chief General Manager of Barclays, did the honours to Dame Cecily and Jack Hulbert, while the rest of us relaxed with the chorus. My partner was a glorious redhead.

London at that time was full of foreign governments. At one cocktail party a distinguished European statesman was loudly maintaining 'Un homme peut couvrir plus de femmes entre l'âge de seize ans et vingt-six ans qu'à aucun autre âge', to which a young woman promptly replied 'Oui, Monsieur le Ministre, couvrir peut-être, mais pas satisfaire.' Years later I quoted to one of that minister's compatriots 'Omne animal post coitum triste', and she at once retorted 'Sauf l'homme et la femme.'

Most people of course were in uniform. Once my mother asked me to tea at the English-Speaking Union. We sat in a huge room and soon a young woman in Air Force blue with 'scrambled egg' on the peak of her cap came and sat in another corner with friends who clearly treated her with some respect. I wanted to leave but my mother insisted on finishing her tea. When she did so and moved to the door, she said in her most piercing tones: 'Isn't that girl in the corner like the Duchess of Gloucester?'

Another feature of wartime London was the Great Fortnum's Chocolate Rush. Sweets were rationed. But it was known that Fortnum's supplies arrived at 2.30 p.m. one day a week. From 2 o'clock that day one could see dowagers fondling teddy-bears and generals busily pushing dolls' prams in the toy department which adjoined the sweet counter. Suddenly the cry went up 'The chocolates are here' and with one accord they abandoned their playthings and charged like elephants across the shop-floor.

But these frivolities soon ended and I was moved, still a GSo3, to Anti-Aircraft Command at Stanmore, where my former divisional general, R. F. E. Whittaker, was now chief of staff. We were close neighbours and collaborators of the RAF Fighter Command at Bentley Priory. So staff-work was now a good deal more serious and substantial, as we were involved in the whole Air Defence of Great

Britain. At this level too the staff comprised some pretty high-powered personalities, most of them only wartime soldiers but none the less efficient for that. I shared a desk and a telephone, for example, with Patrick Buchan-Hepburn who was already an MP of several years' standing and before that had been private secretary to Churchill. He had once dined *à trois* with Winston and Lawrence of Arabia, whom Winston wanted at that time to make Viceroy of India.

This period saw the start of the Baedeker raids on cathedral cities and necessitated much switching of our defences. But my horizons were narrowed again when in mid-1942 I was appointed brigade major of 26th Anti-Aircraft Brigade, responsible for the defences north of the Thames, with an operations room in the former Brompton Road tube station. It was not an easy assignment. On top of other frictions, the Army Council issued an instruction making it possible to retire officers of a certain age who were not up to snuff. This was probably meant for much more active theatres of war; but my brigadier pounced on it to remove one or two regimental commanders who had not found favour. It fell to me to administer the coups de grâce and I was much too young to soften the blow to these elderly gentlemen. Nor, as a bachelor, was I well equipped to deal with all the temperamental problems which seemed to arise from mixed batteries.

On a lighter note, our headquarters were in Hampstead and we used to keep ducks whose eggs could supplement our breakfast rations. One morning we came down and found no eggs. On further investigation we found no ducks. It transpired that a fox had come out of Kenwood and slaughtered them all. This was unexpectedly rustic within three miles of Picadilly Circus.

I suspect it was due to the brigadier's view of my shortcomings that at the end of 1942 I was banished to Northern Ireland as GS02 of the Anti-Aircraft Group there and, in effect, No. 2 to the brigadier in charge. Six months in Ulster offered a strange contrast to wartime London. Belfast had only suffered a couple of serious air-raids and there was little sign of bomb-damage. This was a land without conscription or rationing. I had been given some introductions and one would be invited, as the most natural thing in the world, to four-course dinners served by a butler and two footmen.

There was little sign then of the political and military troubles to come. But one could not fail to be aware that the province was governed by a self-perpetuating Protestant oligarchy, most of whom had been in office since partition in 1922 and had no intention of sharing power with the Catholic minority. They were probably more concerned with the risk of civil unrest and political assassination than with the German menace. Basil Brooke, the then Prime Minister, was a delightful Wykehamist and very welcoming to me, but he refused to employ a single Catholic on his extensive estates. He and his colleagues really did sow the storm and reap the whirlwind.

It was all a little surreal. For example, the Republic of Ireland was said to have formed its air force out of foreign aircraft which had crashed on its territory. By that time it had eleven Spitfires and one Messerschmidt and was only waiting for another Spitfire to crash in order to dispose of the Messerschmidt.

My next move was back to the AA Command staff course, this time as an instructor, the blind leading the blind. This meant lecturing on staff duties and procedure to junior officers who were mostly older than I was and had much more experience of management in civil life. We were housed in Theobald's Park, near Waltham Abbey. The back gate of the estate was, and indeed still is, Temple Bar, which had been moved there many years before from Fleet Street and had fallen into a sad state of disrepair. Efforts to bring it back to the City of London have so far failed to bear fruit. The estate itself had originally belonged to the Cecils, but King James I forced them to swap it for Hatfield, as the hunting was better at Theobald's. It had later belonged to the Meux family, but between the wars had passed into the hands of Mrs. Meyrick, the night-club queen, who turned it into a roadhouse. The bedrooms still bore names like the Confessional or the Nun's Cell, which no doubt somewhat misrepresented the purposes they actually served.

In late summer of 1943, having been selected for the Staff College, I was sent on a preparatory attachment to the Guards Armoured Division in Yorkshire, moving from one unit to another to gain some experience of the various arms. Most of them were billeted in the back premises of large country houses, so that one came to know several of the stately homes of Yorkshire by that access rather than through the front door. With the 5th Coldstream we were subjected to battle training, walking over the moors with bullets whistling at our feet. I have never felt much affection for that neighbourhood since.

The wartime Staff College course was reduced to four months instead of the peacetime two years, and was therefore pretty intensive;

but we could still spend every weekend in London. There was a good deal of paperwork, seminar discussions and simulated war-games. But the highlights were the lectures by distinguished visiting officers. One recent member of the British Military Mission to Moscow claimed to be the only officer of the British army who had seen Marshal Timoshenko dead drunk and Marshal Voroshilov sitting on Stalin's knee. Marshal Timoshenko, incidentally, was supposed to be descended from a Welsh immigrant to Russia called Timothy Jenkins.

General Montgomery came to draw simplified versions of his battles in chalk on the blackboard. These perhaps owed something to hindsight. On Mareth, for example, he claimed that he had been woken in the middle of the night to be told that the Germans were counter-attacking, had told his staff that they should not have woken him but should execute the left-about outflanking hook he had already planned, and had at once gone back to sleep. One of our fellow students, who had been serving at Tac HQ Eighth Army at the time, said that this account bore no relation to the panic which had actually occurred.

The *tour de force* of the whole course was the lecture on the last morning by the Chief of the Imperial General Staff. In an hour, without a note and without pausing for breath, General Alanbrooke took us through all the theatres of war in which British forces were engaged, going into immense detail, even down to the temperature that morning on every front. It was an enormously impressive performance and gave us an object-lesson in what being a staff officer was really all about.

On leaving the Staff College early in 1944, I was posted, again as a GS02, to GHQ AA Troops, which was in practice the anti-aircraft section of Headquarters, 21st Army Group. Our boss was Major-General Bill Revell-Smith, who had two mottoes, which have proved to be invaluable lessons: 'It is always easy to find good reasons for doing nothing' and 'Any fool can be uncomfortable'. Our task was the planning of Overlord, at a time when it was essential to preserve secrecy as to where the invasion was to take place. When one overheard some of the indiscretions committed on the telephone it was astonishing that surprise was eventually achieved. Apart from issuing operational instructions to the anti-aircraft formations under our command, planning mainly concerned the loading of ships in the successive waves of the attack. I remember one morning, when we were demanding shipping-space for our radar sets, the Americans insisted that it was not available as they wanted it for their mobile coffee-roasters.

After D-Day we spent some time in tents in the grounds of St Paul's School at Hammersmith, receiving our baptism of buzz-bombs; but we eventually sailed from Southend for Normandy, long after the battle of the beaches had been won, although there still seemed to be plenty of fireworks around the Mulberry harbours. Apart from dealing with Main HQ 21 Army Group, we also had to communicate with our opposite numbers in Second Army and First Canadian Army, whose headquarters were of course many miles apart. Once I tried to visit both armies in a single journey by jeep, which proved to be far too strenuous and hazardous an undertaking, especially as it meant driving through the area of the recent fighting in the 'Falaise Gap', with the hideous stench of the battlefield still pervading the place.

Soon we were ordered to follow the advance across northern France and we drove into Brussels on the first Sunday after the city was liberated from the Germans. It was quite an occasion. With only two hands it is not easy to drive a jeep, to give the V-sign, to wave at all the pretty girls and to catch the bunches of grapes and bottles of champagne thrown into the vehicle.

We were then allowed to take over any billets which had been occupied by the Germans. One went to the Town Major and asked for quarters for, say, four officers and twenty men. Allotted a house, one inspected it, appropriated the contents of the German army's wine cellar, and returned to the Town Major to report that the house was not entirely suitable and to ask for another. Luckily the Town Major had been a fellow student at the Staff College and we repeated the process until we found luxurious accommodation, then belonging to the Comte de Baillet-Latour and now, I believe, housing the Uruguayan Embassy.

There, I am ashamed to say, we stayed until the end of the war. Apart from the usual staff work, our main direct responsibility was the protection of Brussels from V1s and V2s and liaison with the American Army who were performing the same service for Antwerp. My direct American contact was Bill Edgar, who earned a British Military Cross and who remained one of my dearest friends until his death early in 1990. The only other excitement occurred at dawn on New Year's Day 1945, when I was walking home from a dance and met the Luftwaffe machine-gunning below the level of the rooftops. The Rundstedt offensive had begun in the Ardennes and for a short while all was panic and pandemonium.

Otherwise the war seemed very far from Brussels that winter. Once shortly before Christmas I was summoned to a conference at Chatham. There was thick fog and our pilot had difficulty in finding somewhere to land. Eventually, with darkness falling, no blind-flying gear and ten minutes' petrol left, we came down at a lonely airfield called Harwell. No doubt atomic bombs were being invented in the Nissen hut at the end of the runway. At least there were no customs as we were all carrying contraband presents for our families. At Chatham next day, again delayed by fog, I was given profuse apologies that the meeting had started without me and ushered into the room. There was an admiral of the fleet, a dozen other naval officers none below the rank of commodore, two air vice-marshals and an air commodore; I then realised that Major Barnes was representing the army. Admiral Tovey turned to me: 'We are so sorry not to have waited; for your benefit we shall recapitulate what we have said so far.' Luckily the flag lieutenant had fortified me with a quick pink gin.

After VE Day I managed to detach myself from the headquarters, together with a truck and driver, batman and despatch-rider all my own. We did not feature on any establishment but as we were self-contained seemed to be welcome wherever we went. The despatch-rider's only duty was to take our tea ration, find the nearest American unit and exchange the tea for coffee. I still see regularly the staff sergeant and bombardier clerk of those days.

The problem was what to do with ourselves for the rest of our amateur soldiering. I could have done some sort of garrison duty in occupied Germany, but I wanted something more interesting and eventually succeeded in joining the North German Coal Control, which was part of the Control Commission administering the British Zone. Germany was already rising like a phoenix from some very flattened ashes and coal was the key to her rise. It was fascinating to see the rebirth from nothing of a modern industrial economy, as German entrepreneurs would apply for ten tons of coal to start a sugar refinery, a hundred tons for a steelworks or a thousand tons for a power station. One began to see the bones being put together into a skeleton and then growing flesh again. We were only to learn later that we in Britain had not been bombed enough; the nations of continental Europe had suffered so much that they started again way behind us but moved with such speed and determination that they soon overtook us, while much of Britain remained a nineteenth-century industrial museum.

The headquarters of the NGCC was in the Villa Hügel, Herr Krupp's grandiose mansion near Essen. The owner was otherwise engaged in a prison camp, awaiting trial at Nuremberg, which he eventually escaped on health grounds. Here I tried to learn the rudiments of coal production. The population of the British Zone was fed on a ration scale designed to be adequate to avoid 'disease and unrest'. But feeding miners on those rations would not have dug much coal and we had to secure them more calories. This generated a good deal of jealousy and when I applied for a supply of cold cream, I was laughed out of court as pampering my clients until I explained that anyone who had been down a coalmine would know that there was no other way of cleaning up afterwards. I had myself been down to see the famous German coal-plough in action, except that it shot past generating such a noise and such a cloud of coaldust that one could not observe it at all. Even so, we had a good deal of trouble persuading the miners to work for us, until one day there was a ghastly accident in which over 400 men were killed; the senior British controllers, who were all pitmen themselves, left their desks and went down below to help in the rescue work. From then on the miners realised that we were all working to the same end and the whole atmosphere changed.

The Americans had occupied the Villa Hügel before us and had apparently stripped it of anything interesting. But one day one of our number knocked on a wall, heard a hollow sound, broke down an entrance and found all Herr Krupp's best wine stored away. That hock lasted us several months.

Soon I transferred to the Economic Section of the Control Commission at Bad Oeynhausen to take charge of coal allocation from there. This was at the invitation of Michael Berry, who had been a colleague at GHQ AA Troops and who wanted a successor so that he could return to the *Daily Telegraph*. It was a sad day when, some forty years later, by now Lord Hartwell, he had control of his beloved newspaper wrested from his grasp. He told me once, soon after the war, that in the captured German archives it was found that his father, Lord Camrose, had been marked for immediate arrest 'because he had allowed his family to marry the descendants of an oriental tribe'. This was because Michael's sister-in-law, Lady Eleanor Smith, daughter of F. E., had written entirely fanciful reminiscences, claiming descent from gypsies.

For her powerful imagination, if Hitler had won, the whole family would no doubt have gone straight to a concentration camp or worse.

Being in charge of coal allocation, I gave myself a ration of ten tons a month. It was worth its weight in gold then and had I sold it I need never have worked again . But it had to be dumped on the pavement outside my quarters and I used to lie awake at night, listening to the Germans diligently shovelling it away.

A more tangible benefit came from persuading my colleagues that I must travel to Vienna to buy pitprops for my North German coalmines. This involved a splendid sightseeing drive right across Germany and more sightseeing in Vienna itself. The city was in a sad state: the Stefansdom under repair and no roof on the Kunsthistorisches Museum. But the best pictures were to be seen in the Hofburg. At the end of the war Baldur von Schirach, Gauleiter of Vienna, had the bright idea of transferring these masterpieces to the German 'national redoubt' in Bavaria. General Mark Clark set off in pursuit and a pitched battle ensued at a crossroads, with machine-gun bullets whizzing between the packing-cases. Miraculously, the canvases emerged unscathed. Or at any rate that was the story.

On the way to Vienna we passed through Nuremberg and I tried to get into the court, without success. Goering was in the witness box and the courtroom was said to be packed. But I did spend a day at the Belsen trial, where my main impression was the obvious and complete absence of any trace of regret or repentance on the face of Irma Grese, the notorious wardress. Instead, she was said to spend her time signalling to friends in the audience how badly she wanted a man.

I also managed a trip to Berlin that winter. General Monty had expressed a wish to travel there by train. But as the Russians were removing railway-lines as reparations, no one knew if a passable track still existed. So it was decided to send a guinea-pig train first, with expendable passengers like Barnes, across the Soviet Zone. Not knowing whether we were going to plunge into the Elbe, we sat up drinking champagne and playing poker in a well-lit carriage. At one stop the Russian soldiery thought they would like to join in the fun, until our military police guards started to shoot over their heads. So we arrived safely in the shattered capital.

When not travelling, we used to ride horses at Minden. They belonged to some Russian DPs (displaced persons); so the horses were presumably DHs. They were lively animals until the time came for men and horses to be sent back to Russia, no doubt there to be liquidated, although we did not know it at the time. Before they left, the Russians begged us to take them on a tour of Gamburg and Ganover. It is well known that Shakespeare was a Russian author who wrote *Gamlet*. I am sorry we could not do them that last favour.

Bizarre things happened in Germany in those days. One of the most bizarre befell an American friend, Rebecca Wellington, who was serving with a War Crimes Investigation Unit in Marburg. Late one night the doorbell rang. They unbolted the door to find a top sergeant of the US Army who asked if this was Unit No 12345, as he had a parcel for them, for which they must sign in triplicate. This done, he threw a parcel on the floor and disappeared into the night. They then found that they had signed for 'Bones of the Prussian Kings' and there on the floor lay the mortal remains of Frederick the Great, Frederick William IV and President and Frau von Hindenburg, whom the Americans in Berlin had decided must be rescued from the clutches of the advancing Russian hordes. The two monarchs could later be accommodated in the family vaults at Burg Hohenzollern. But the Hindenburgs, who stemmed from East Prussia, had no such luck and to this day they remain in the Elisabethkirche at Marburg, which they had never visited in their lifetimes. By 1990 it was planned to send Frederick the Great, at any rate, back to Potsdam, to redress the balance of history.

Apart from such excitements, we led a comfortable life, sending a lorry to Denmark if we wanted caviar or a truck to Reims if we needed champagne. Not since the Middle Ages had Europe been so free from frontiers at least for the occupying forces. Let us hope that something of the kind will return in 1993. But even so it was an artificial and dead-end existence to masquerade as a coal-merchant in uniform. So I was not sorry to be demobilised in the spring of 1946.

Oh, what an inglorious war and what a waste of nearly seven years of my life.

4
Diplomatic Début

No more deadly form of literature can be found than diplomatic memoirs. My great-grandfather, who was Minister-Resident to the Hanse Towns until Bismarck absorbed them into the German Empire in 1870, wrote a totally unreadable book, dropping names which are long since forgotten and resurrecting controversies which were far better buried. The only other memento of him is a scrap of paper in Palmerston's handwriting: 'I wish Mr Ward would write a little larger.' It takes the pen of a Harold Nicolson to make such memories fictitious and therefore funny.

Emerging from the war with no distinctions or qualifications whatever and having been accepted before it as a fit person to take the Foreign Office examination, I followed the line of least resistance and duly presented myself. Luckily they called it a reconstruction examination and tempered the wind to the shorn lamb who had hardly read a serious book for seven years. They were looking more for native wit than learning. To prepare for it, however, I read Fisher's *History of Europe* and Keynes's *General Theory of Employment, Interest and Money*. At least it led to employment and plenty of interest, but very little money.

After it was over, and I had survived a so-called weekend house party at Stoke D'Abernon, I was summoned by the Head of the Foreign Office Personnel Department, who told me I was being sent to Washington. Innocently, I asked what I should do there. A foolish question deserves a foolish answer, which was 'You'll need a white dinner-jacket and you'll have to drink a lot of whisky. Goodbye.' They were the only instructions I ever received for a diplomatic career, quite good as far as they went, but not perhaps going quite far enough. Probably more apposite was Moley Sargent, as Permanent Under-Secretary, who, when a colleague complained of frustration, wearily replied: 'But surely you know that all we are paid to do is to plough the sand.'

The journey to the United States took place in an antique Cunarder still fitted up as a troopship. That was not the only discomfort. The voyage lasted ten days. We only had one storm: it also lasted ten days. On sailing into New York, we were greeted by a huge sign reading 'Uneeda Biscuit'. I could have done with something stronger.

At Washington they took one look at me and ordered 'Write the Weekly Economic Summary.' I had never been in the United States before, had only read one book on economics and had never written a Foreign Office telegram. In despair I turned to the Economic Section on page 95 of the *New York Times,* copied out two columns and served them up. Luckily, none of my superiors had read beyond page 94.

Washington at the end of 1946 was a fascinating place. The mid-term congressional elections had just been held. The posters were still in place: 'Had enough? Vote Republican.' The Republicans had duly won. For the first time in twenty years the President was faced with a Congress of the opposing party. Two years later this was to lead the media pundits to write off Truman's chances of re-election. They reckoned without their man. He 'gave them hell' and he got back into the White House. Not only was he a man of decision; he knew what the people wanted. He also had the personal touch and it did a great deal for the morale of a very junior diplomat, at a White House reception for the diplomatic corps, which then only numbered a few hundred, to have his name announced and to be greeted by a little man standing on a footstool, to bring his height up to his wife's, who at once said 'Good evening, Mr Barnes. This is Mr Barnes, my dear.' Admittedly, it probably helped to follow on a colleague in full Arab dress with an unpronounceable name.

But Washington under Truman was just waking up to be the capital of the Western world. The euphoria of the Roosevelt years and of the flirtation with 'Uncle Joe' was fading, had already fast faded. Winston Churchill had proclaimed the Iron Curtain, at first much to American annoyance; but he was right and the Cold War had begun. There followed in rapid succession the Truman Doctrine for Greece and Turkey, the Marshall Plan for Europe and, following the second defenestration of Prague, the North Atlantic Treaty. Under Truman the United States was choosing its corner and exerting its leadership. It was of course a time of bipartisanship in foreign policy, thanks largely to the wisdom and responsibility of Senator Vandenberg on the Republican side. In London, too, at that time there was a broad cross-party consensus on foreign affairs: Bevin probably had more trouble with his own back benchers than with the Conservative opposition. As Germany was occupied and France still recovering from occupation, it fell to the Anglo-American partnership, the so-called special relationship, to weld the West together to resist further soviet penetration. Anthony Eden used to talk of the three interlocking circles: the British Commonwealth, Europe and the Anglo-American link-up. But, although in the Foreign Office some consideration was given to trying to form a third world power, based on a European-Commonwealth network under British leadership, it soon became clear that the only feasible policy was Western consolidation involving full American participation. Europe was still war weary and weak, both economically and militarily, and the movement for political unity was in its infancy, sustained only by the still small voice of Jean Monnet. The Commonwealth was already showing more signs of division than of unity: political, economic and military purposes were aimed in widely diverging, if not actually conflicting, directions. In geographical terms alone, even the Commonwealth countries of that time could not be expected to follow a coordinated path. Only an effort to bring the policies of all non-Communist countries into harmony, however loosely orchestrated, could be expected to dispel Soviet dreams of global domination.

My own involvement in these great events was minor and marginal. I went to the State Department with Donald Maclean, of whom more anon, to open the negotiations for handing over to the US Government our responsibilities in respect of Greece and Turkey. I also took a lowly part in the arrangements to amalgamate the British and American Zones of Germany into a so-called bizone. When General Marshall in June 1947 made his Harvard speech, which led to the Plan named after him, it was again Donald Maclean who asked me, then working on economic matters, to tell a journalist friend of his what we thought of the speech. I told the man from *US News and World Report* that, if he did not attribute anything to the British Embassy, I would give him our first reactions, and pretty primitive they were. Next week, thinking no evil but detecting a certain excitement in the Embassy, I found that a telegram was about to go to London reporting the private views of President Truman and Secretary Marshall on aid to Europe. This was based on an article in *US News and World Report*, where all my brash comments had been ascribed to the President and Secretary of State.

My confession succeeded in stopping the telegram. When I remonstrated with the journalist, he said in the words of W. S. Gilbert: 'I had to give verisimilitude to an otherwise bald and unconvincing narrative and you only said I was not to attribute it to the Embassy.' I had been warned.

The British Embassy was already a vast institution with different members specialising in every aspect of international affairs. Americans used to say to us that we seemed to have people dealing with every other part of the world, but no one apparently dealing with the United States. Certainly one's hostess at a cocktail party would say 'You two must know each other; you are both at the British Embassy' and one would shake hands with someone one had never consciously seen before.

Over it all the time I was there, presided our Ambassador, Archie Clark Kerr, by then Lord Inverchapel. He was a man of great experience, with a long and successful career behind him, although by now perhaps a little tired. But he still exercised great charm, not only in his handling of foreign statesmen but also his kindness to raw newcomers. Perhaps he made friends almost too easily. But he had his austere moments too. At the King's Birthday Party in 1947, a time of acute dollar shortage, he decided to serve only soft drinks in the heat of a Washington summer; *Life* magazine came out with pictures of wilting guests in the Embassy garden and the caption: 'Never have so many sweated so much for so little.'

As a true Scot, Inverchapel had his own piper, who would play round the table after dinner, close behind the diners in that not over-large dining-room, whereat the guests would remark pointedly how delightful the pipes sounded at the end of a garden. He also had his own Russian valet. The story, as I remember hearing it from Inverchapel himself, although it has been told differently elsewhere, was that, on leaving Moscow after his highly successful wartime mission, he paid his farewell call on Molotov, then Foreign Minister, who sang his praises and offered him vast quantities of vodka, caviar or some other suitable tribute. Inverchapel replied that he only had one request, which he was sure Molotov would refuse: he would like to take with him the manservant who had served him well. 'You are quite right,' said Molotov 'the answer is nyet.' Next day Inverchapel went to say goodbye to Stalin: more offers of generous farewell gifts but Inverchapel repeated his request and Molotov's answer. Stalin replied

'Molotov always says nyet', summoned the Foreign Minister and told him to issue the exit visa. Needless to say, when this moujik turned up in Washington, the Americans assumed he was a Russian spy; but in fact, his interests, as he patrolled the servants' floor of the Embassy, were understood to be more physical than political.

Years earlier, as Minister at Santiago, Clark Kerr had married the daughter of the President of Chile, some thirty years younger than himself. They had parted company in China; but he remained devoted to her and, when it was suggested to him that an Ambassadress would be an asset in Washington, he remarried his former wife. She added greatly to the vivacity of the establishment and was soon a lively figure on the Washington social scene, not much older than we second secretaries. It was therefore all the sadder that it was soon decided in London that the time had come for the Ambassador to retire and be replaced by Oliver Franks, who was more familiar with current economic problems and had indeed been the architect on the receiving end of the Marshall Plan. Although Inverchapel himself put a brave face on it, saying that he looked forward to returning to his Highland sheep, his wife made no secret of her disappointment and her lack of interest in sheep.

There were other colourful characters in the Embassy, notably Jock Balfour, the Minister, who wrote one of the most light-hearted but shrewd of diplomatic memoirs. But in any picture of the British Embassy at Washington in the years immediately after the war, the controversial figure of Donald Maclean inevitably looms large. Not that he was in any way controversial then. On the contrary, as many of his colleagues were to say after his disappearance, he was widely regarded as the *beau idéal* of a diplomatist, having both ability and charm in equally generous measures.

This is not the place to attempt yet another estimate of his personality and his actions. Many pages and more than one book have already been written about him. The usual cliché is to describe him as Dr Jekyll and Mr Hyde. Certainly he seems to have been able to switch almost effortlessly from one mode to another. All I can say is that I never met Mr Hyde.

In Washington not only did I work quite closely with Donald Maclean; he was also extremely kind to me. He has been called arrogant. But he tutored a green and ignorant neophyte in the mysteries of diplomacy with great gentleness, taking me, as I have said, as his assistant to open the negotiations at the State Department for what became the Truman Doctrine for the support of Greece and Turkey, when Britain could no longer carry that burden. He patiently explained me responsibilities of the various members of that huge Embassy, including, ironically, his own functions with regard to atomic matters, which were then highly secret but were later to attract so much obloquy. If, as a footloose bachelor, I went to the office on a Sunday, he was often hard at work at his desk, with two-year-old Fergie crawling round the floor, but always ready to break off and discuss any problem with patient courtesy. He had a fine analytical mind, well-stored with specific examples to illustrate general propositions.

Donald and Melinda also welcomed me into their home. Many a night did I play bridge with them, often with Melinda's mother, Mrs. Dunbar, as the fourth, often until the early hours of the morning. But never did I see Donald the worse for drink. Indeed, once when Cynthia and I went with him to Glen Echo, the amusement park outside Washington, where the terrifying giant roller-coaster caused us to cling together so closely that we felt we had to be married after that, Donald was waiting for us at the bottom with nothing to restore our morale but a can of root-beer, a singularly nauseating non-alcoholic drink. Even before that, our first evening out together had been at the Dancing Class, a rather élite subscription dance club, for which we borrowed Melinda's mink coat. We passed most of the evening commuting between the dance-floor and the cloakroom to make sure the coat had not been stolen.

These are only trivial examples of Maclean's generosity to someone to whom he owed nothing. Then it was certainly Dr Jekyll all the way. On my last day in Washington in 1948 he even asked me to luncheon and drove me to the station. Although I had meanwhile met his mother, a gentle lady with strong liberal and reformist views, I did not see Donald again until we were both working in the Foreign Office in 1950. This was after his turbulent time in Cairo, where Mr Hyde had certainly raised his ugly head, though quite unbeknown to me and most of our colleagues. I saw him occasionally in the way of business, particularly at the time of Attlee's visit to Washington in December 1950 when he, as head of the American Department, was naturally concerned with the briefs which I was co-ordinating. He was as usual calm, debonair and helpful. In May 1951, for no particular reason that

I can remember, except that I liked him and was grateful for his kindness, I asked him to luncheon at my club. We talked, as colleagues do, about current policy; he certainly spoke admiringly of Wilfrid Scawen Blunt's opposition to British 'imperialism' in Egypt under Cromer and he asked rhetorically what good we thought we were doing to the Korean people by chasing backwards and forwards across their country in armoured vehicles. But this was all calm, sober and good-humoured. There was no suggestion of Communist fanaticism; it seemed a not unusual case of one bureaucrat letting off to another a little private steam about policies which he had to execute but with which he did not whole-heartedly agree. Certainly I suspected nothing. How naive can you be? I was naive in good company. Better men than I were equally unsuspicious. Neither then nor at any other time did he so much as hint that he was sounding me out as a possible recruit to his cause, although by then it would have been too late for him to do so anyway. Nor, perhaps I should say in view of later allegations as to his behaviour, did he ever make anything remotely resembling a pass at me.

After that luncheon, his disappearance ten days later came as all the greater shock to those of us who thought we knew him well. It did not make it any better that he had gone with Burgess, whom I had met once or twice in the office and found a most unprepossessing individual. Apart from the public aspects, our first private reaction was one of sympathy for Melinda. So the shock was redoubled when a couple of years later she went the self-same way. In neither case did the news of the flight reach the powers that be until it was too late to organise an effective pursuit; each time the fugitives held the initiative. Inevitably there was talk of a cover-up, but if so it was the fugitives or their accomplices covering their own tracks, not the authorities wishing good riddance to bad rubbish.

But it is still the enigma of Donald Maclean which sticks in the gullet. Dr Jekyll and Mr Hyde? Or were there three Macleans: the *preux chevalier*, the Communist agent and what would now be called the lager lout? It is tempting to surmise that the lager lout only emerged when the conflict between the first two *personae* became too hot to handle. But the drinking bouts seem to have originated before any such conflict could have arisen. It has also been suggested that the left-wing ideas and the personal indiscipline constituted a reaction against a teetotal, nonconformist, authoritarian father, combined with the anti-fascist atmosphere of Cambridge in the thirties. But, if so, why such an extreme reaction? Many of us were subjected to the same, or similar, influences. But we did not go overboard. Were we too cynical? Had we imbibed with our classical studies the doctrine of μηδὲν ἄγαν, moderation in all things? Did we lack the courage of our convictions? Certainly, few of us would have had the consummate ability to lead a double life and escape detection for so long as Maclean did.

So it would be going too far, in contemplating the course of Donald Maclean's life, to say 'there, but for the grace of God, went I'. The resulting emotion is certainly not relief. Nor is it only anger that we were deceived and the country betrayed, although that must play its part. Looking back, one sees above all the tragedy of so much promise wasted. I feel very sad.

One would like to think that there might be a consolation. Is it possible that Maclean continued to be asked for advice by at least some members of the Soviet leadership? If so, could that advice have been on the side of moderation? Could he, for example, have urged that the Soviet Government would never achieve its desired objectives, particularly in the economic field, if it continued to present the unacceptable face of Communism to the world? In that case, can Maclean be regarded as partially and indirectly responsible for *glasnost* and *perestroika*? Is this wishful thinking?

But these unhappy events were then still in the future. Life in Washington, though busy and stimulating, was also remarkably carefree. There was little or no hierarchical stuffiness in the conduct of business. A second secretary could correspond directly with a United States Senator. Nor was there any rank consciousness in the Embassy itself. My senior colleagues were approachable, generous and welcoming. I could entertain easily in my little house in Georgetown, although still very naive and ignorant of what diplomatic duties required. The pound sterling was still worth four dollars and, although Detroit was not yet back to full postwar production, one could acquire a powerful Chevrolet for $1,200 and a judiciously placed case of whisky.

One's sense of purpose was enhanced by working in the almost monumental Embassy building on Massachusetts Avenue, disfigured though it was by the hastily constructed wartime annexe next door. Lady Lindsay, who had been the first Ambassadress to occupy it in the 1930s, was to tell us tales of Lutyens's little ways in designing it.

Although he sometimes erred, as when putting the wine-cellar next to the heating boiler, he took great pains over details, sitting on every loo and stretching out a hand to show just where the paper should be hung. The entrance to the house was tiled rather frigidly in black and white and there was then a long corridor to the main drawing-room. When Lady Lindsay protested at this chilling and forbidding approach, Lutyens replied: 'Dear Lady, I did not want anyone to feel any warmth in this house until they came into the presence of their hostess.' To which she retorted: 'Being an American I have been asked to do a great many things as a British Ambassadress, but never before have I been asked to be the central heating system.'

Washington had some other lighter moments. Once, walking downtown, I noticed that the flags were flying at half-mast and, as a trained Englishman, asked a policeman the reason. 'Oh', he said, 'I guess they couldn't be bothered to pull them up any higher.' Another time I was standing at a street corner opposite a sign saying 'DON'T WALK'. At the appropriate moment, DON'T was supposed to disappear and you walked. On this occasion WALK disappeared and I hastily inspected myself to see what I was doing that I shouldn't.

Sadly, my short time in Washington never took me far from the East Coast. But even with that limitation there was plenty to see within the distance of a weekend's motoring, which sometimes meant driving through Sunday night for a quick champagne breakfast before appearing at one's desk at 9 a.m. on Monday morning. One particularly happy retreat was the home near Kingston, NY, of Mrs Francie Leggett, in whose house, when she was Mrs David Margesson, I had attended dancing classes twenty-five years earlier. She was a generous person of pronounced enthusiasms and at this time was particularly interested in helping German refugees. We had to have our meals on the verandah because Duke Odo of Württemberg was celebrating mass in the dining-room. A cottage was occupied by Ruth Fischer, sister of Gerhard Eisler, who had defected from the West to become Minister of Information in East Germany; she was intent on proving that Stalin's policies were recapitulating those of Hitler and would rush into the room proclaiming that they were just about to burn the Reichstag, or occupy the Rhineland. In another cottage was Gottfried Treviranus, Minister of Transport in Bruening's Weimar government, and his beautiful daughter, Barbara, now married to Friedrich Adler. There was never a dull moment in that establishment, which was also full of Francie Leggett's English family. When we were not arguing heatedly on politics, we might be weeding corn, throwing boomerangs or bathing at midnight in puris naturalibus.

Barbara Treviranus, by the way, had been in the family house in the Grünewald in Berlin on 30 June 1934, with her father playing tennis on the court at the end of the garden. The door bell rang and she answered it, to find two S.S. men with revolvers at the ready. 'Where is your father?' 'I do not know.' 'Oh yes, you do. We are taking you round the house with a gun in your back until you lead us to him.' She managed to press a button which rang on the tennis court, whereupon her father without further ado vaulted the garden wall. By sheer good luck there he found a Catholic priest with whom he exchanged his tennis clothes for a soutane and, thus accoutred, escaped from Germany to England, where he was befriended by Robert Vansittart. Barbara herself and her mother managed to leave Germany a little later by the simple but dangerous expedient of taking a cruise and, when the ship docked at London, walking down the gangplank to freedom. The family had then spent the war years in Canada.

But my days in Washington were numbered and were to last less than eighteen months. During 1947 William Strang came over as head of two successive missions from Berlin, where he was Political Adviser to the Commander-in-Chief, to enlist American cooperation in the administration of occupied Germany. I was attached to him to give local support. Each time he brought his private secretary and, as William sat in his office every night until 4 a.m. drafting telegrams which, given the time difference, would then arrive in London just as the Foreign Office opened for business, that private secretary and I had nothing to do but sit in the outer office and get engaged to each other.

So I asked the Foreign Office for leave to be married in London and for two passages then to be booked back to Washington. No such luck. They were not prepared to pay dollars for two people in Washington and I was to be transferred to a home appointment.

5
Worm's-Eye View

Diplomats are employed to deal with foreigners. But inevitably, over the years one came in touch with Foreign Secretaries and Prime Ministers of both parties in one's own country. One is often asked 'Who was the best Foreign Secretary you knew?' and sometimes 'Who was the worst?' Comparisons are odious, and in this case impertinent and way beyond my competence. I can only offer the odd glimpse from the worm's eye.

It would not be too much to say that Ernest Bevin was loved by many of his officials, partly no doubt because he was so much closer to their own views than they had expected. He did not try to outsmart diplomats at their own game; he applied rugged commonsense and solid patriotism, which usually produced the right answers. Of course, he remained a socialist; confronted by a despatch quoting political gossip dripped into an Ambassador's ear by a President's mistress, or some such authority, Bevin scrawled across it: 'What do the workers think?' But, socialist or not, he was not starry-eyed about Stalinist Russia. Indeed, there was not much love lost by that time between British socialists and Stalin, who was reputed to prefer Beaverbrook's company to Cripps's; perhaps one can see why. From the start Bevin was determined to build up Western security: he took the lead in breaking the Berlin blockade and concluding the Dunkirk and Brussels Treaties, leading on to NATO. Despite his humble origins, leadership was in his blood, well spiced with humour. He came to Washington while I was there and addressed the assembled Embassy: 'You could run the Foreign Service without me. But I couldn't run it without you. To begin with, I can't type.' Unluckily, I only saw him at close quarters at the end of his life. He was tired and the glory had departed a bit. I had to help with one or two of his parliamentary speeches. We all offered advice until he said 'Send for a clerk' and the excellent and diminiutive Alison David came in with pencil and pad. We then had to reassemble his dictation into coherent form and were still doing so, with sheets of paper all over the floor, when he had to move to the Front Bench. I can remember him staggering, or rather rolling, along to the Chamber, clutching our sheaves with him, obviously at the end of his tether. Then some intervention by Harold Macmillan provoked him into a cataract of his invective, with the text we had laboured to prepare quite forgotten. The end was sad; at a meeting in the Cabinet room to prepare for Attlee's visit to Truman in December, 1950, Bevin, whose doctors had forbidden him to travel by air with the Prime Minister, vented his disappointment on the whole enterprise with nothing but destructive comments. It was obvious that he could not long continue and within a few weeks he was dead.

One aspect of Bevin's policy, which later came to haunt me, was his attitude to Palestine and Israel. He was accused of being anti-semitic: there were stories of a conflict years earlier with a Jewish trade-unionist whom he had particularly disliked. He was certainly capable of strong personal animosities, as when someone said that Nye Bevan was his own worst enemy and Ernie answered 'Not while I'm alive, he isn't.' Certainly, too, the American Jewish community believed in his anti-semitism. A fortnight before I reached Washington late in 1946, during the United Nations debates, a grandson of Theodor Herzl, the founder of Zionism, had flung himself from the Massachusetts Avenue bridge a few hundred yards from our Embassy, almost certainly some kind of political gesture. During the ensuing months, too, the Embassy was constantly telephoned with bomb threats, so that we had to evacuate the building and try to do our work in the garden, our papers fluttering round our ears. But in fairness to Bevin, he was no doubt convinced that handing over Palestine to the United Nations served British interests better than continuing the Mandate. Certainly his biographer, Alan Bullock, concluded in effect that Bevin's hostility to the Jews derived from the policy he felt himself obliged to follow rather than vice versa. Moreover, the Arabs outnumbered the Jews and, for one who had always dealt in massive trade union bloc votes, God was on the side of the big battalions. This would also have been in line with his advice from officials But the Israelis have never forgotten nor forgiven.

Indeed, if the two worst mistakes of British foreign policy since the war were the Suez adventure and the failure to join the European Community at the right time, a third may well have been our failure to bring Israel into the Commonwealth in or around 1948. Admittedly, the atmosphere then was not propitious and we had suffered from violent Jewish resistance. But we did not later strain at the camel of welcoming Kenya after the Mau-Mau, Cyprus after EOKA or Zimbabwe after UDI. Israel would have been a gnat by comparison. With Israel at that time we might also have brought in Jordan, perhaps Iraq and possibly even Egypt, all more or less post-colonial situations. If so, the whole subsequent course of events in the Middle East might well have been dramatically changed and the Suez mistake would never have been committed. But the might-have-beens of history are never rewarding subjects for speculation.

Bevin was succeeded by Herbert Morrison. There was no love lost between the two men and Morrison as Foreign Secretary was undoubtedly actuated in part by a desire to be different from Bevin, to whom he may have suspected the Foreign Office was unduly loyal. This was not only true of his Middle Eastern policy, in which he was much more in the pro-Zionist mainstream tradition of the Labour Party. After all, the Israeli leadership at that time was firmly and exclusively socialist, when most other countries in the region were feudal monarchies. This, incidentally, was surely one reason why Russia recognised Israel as quickly as she did. But Bevin in his anti-Zionism had been a maverick in his own party, just as Winston Churchill, as a self-proclaimed Zionist, was at odds with most Conservative thinking. One of Bevin's bitterest opponents on his own back-benches over Palestine had been Dick Crossman. I soon found myself writing Morrison's speeches and was instructed to do so in collaboration with his PPS (later Lord) Shackleton, who at the time was sharing a flat with Crossman. It would be unworthy to suggest that the pen of Shackleton had been dipped in the venom of Crossman. But certainly the political input to the speeches was often hard to reconcile with the mainline thinking of my Foreign Office superiors.

There came a time when Morrison said that as I wrote the speeches, I had better hear one. So we set off for the Midlands. First he visited Mrs Morrison in hospital. So we missed the train at Euston. We dashed across London and were ushered into a carriage by the Paddington station-master in a top hat. After that, Birmingham was rather a come-down: at Snow Hill station we were met by the local party agent in an elderly raincoat and a mini-car. We then stopped for a drink at every party committee-room in the area, before arriving a couple of hours late for the meeting at Dudley, where George Wigg, the local member, had been valiantly keeping the audience in play. Morrison told me to listen from the body of the hall, and, as I crept to my seat in the then Foreign Office uniform of blue suit, stiff white collar, black hat and red Cabinet box, Morrison appeared on the platform and the whole audience burst into song with the 'Red Flag'. I felt as if I could have sunk through the floor, like someone in a Bateman drawing.

After the meeting we repaired to the Queen's Hotel at Birmingham, where the local Party had reserved a suite with vast sitting-room. Morrison took one look and asked 'What do they think I am, a member of the bloody *bourgeoisie*?' A waiter appeared, looking and sounding like Mischa Auer, the film star, and inquired in languid tones: 'Would you like soupe vichyssoise and sole véronique done with grapes?' Morrison looked him up and down and demanded 'Fried fish and chips'; so we sat down together to that, washed down with lashings of whisky, while Morrison regaled me with indiscretions about his colleagues. He claimed, by the way, to be a Cockney, but on that I could trump him, as the Temple is much nearer Bow Bells than Brixton is.

Next morning he breakfasted in that suite, while the detective and I went down. The head waiter, in those rationed days, told us there were kippers, kippers and kippers on the menu, then bent low and murmured 'But there's egg and bacon for you.' Never have I felt more like a commissar.

Herbert Morrison was very kind to me, but that did not make him an outstanding Foreign Secretary. On his first day in office, he was reported to have sent for the life of Palmerston. But he did not share that minister's power of decision. William Strang, as Permanent Secretary, used to complain that if one submitted two alternative courses of action and asked Morrison to approve one of them his reply would be to the effect that '(a) is well worth consideration but there is also much to be said for (b).'

Towards the end of his time at the Foreign Office, he was pitchforked into the troubles over Mossadeq and Persian oil. My task at the time was to brief the Lord Chancellor for foreign affairs debates in the House of Lords. This was a nightmare. Jowitt was a masterly advocate but his knowledge of foreign affairs was, to say the least, limited. He would listen carefully to advice beforehand but in the House was liable to be carried away by his own eloquence. On this occasion the Prime Minister had ended a Commons debate the night before with the words 'We shall not leave Abadan'. This begged a number of questions and Lord Salisbury opened next day's Lords debate by asking for more details of the Government's plans. I went out to consult Morrison and Richard Stokes, the Minister conducting the negotiations, and was told to advise Jowitt to stick strictly to the Prime Minister's words and no more. By the elaborate method of attracting the attention of an attendant in full evening dress with a gilt chain on his ample midriff and handing him a scribbled note to convey to the Woolsack, I passed this advice on to the Lord Chancellor. Jowitt, used to addressing juries, repeated Attlee's words all right but then, to add verisimilitude to what he obviously considered a bald and unconvincing narrative, he added, 'We stand by that statement, we stand by all the implications of that statement' and so on. This potential military commitment could have got the Government into deep water, but luckily the Opposition did not pursue it.

Attlee himself, in his quiet way, exercised great authority and a calm mastery of foreign affairs. If he had to wind up a debate, he would listen attentively to our suggestions from all round the room. But he did not accept official advice uncritically. His political antennae were sharply switched on. After listening, he would set down, precisely and succinctly, the main themes of the debate and the main points he intended to make in reply. From there it was fairly easy to construct a lucid speech and he would stick quite closely to it.

But the closest I saw of him in action was in December 1950, when there were fears that the Americans might drop the atomic bomb in Korea and Attlee decided to fly at short notice to Washington. This blew up during a foreign affairs debate; before it ended, President Truman's agreement to receive the Prime Minister and the King's permission for his absence had to be secured, so that the House could be informed in the winding-up speech. If fell to my lot to draft a message to the President and then to coordinate the briefs for the visit. As a result, I was lucky enough to be told to take the record of the meetings in the Oval Office, where there must have been fewer than twenty people present. Truman was most impressive. He had mastered his briefs and spoke to them with vigour and humour. Also, experienced politician that he was, he never entered or left the room without shaking hands with everyone in it, including the humble minute-writer.

The President was flanked on his right by General Marshall, Secretary of Defense, and on his left by the Secretary of State, Dean

Acheson, both legendary figures. At one point of the discussion on Korea, Acheson was arguing that the United States should 'lean up against China'. It was not entirely clear what he meant, but Marshall at once retorted that you could put the whole American army into China and lose it in two weeks. We British were silent spectators of this internal American exchange, listening while the mighty diplomatist advocated forceful action and the powerful soldier counselled caution. Incidentally, it was at that meeting that General Eisenhower's appointment as NATO Supreme Commander was formally agreed.

It was fascinating to watch Oliver Franks, the distinguished moral philosopher who was then our Ambassador, in action. The two leaders argued about various controversial matters during the day. At the end of the session, the Ambassador might say: 'Mr President, Mr Prime Minister do you think we might put it this way . . . ?' and then with considerable dexterity he would spin a web of words which allowed everyone to go home convinced that they all agreed with each other. Sometimes, in the cold light of dawn, it became clear that there was still a gulf to be bridged and the argument must start again.

The sequel to that visit to Washington was, as usual with Prime Ministers, a return via Ottawa. Field-Marshal Alexander was Governor-General and nobly put the library cum billiard-room of Government House at our disposal as an office. Some of our delegation, such as Field-Marshal Slim and Roger Makins, were rather larger than life and seemed to take up the whole place. The rest of us huddled in corners. Then Attlee came in and said he had a speech to prepare. We offered to draft it. 'No. Give me a typewriter. I am not a very good typist. But I like to do it myself.' So there, amid those mighty men striding around, at a typewriter on a card table, sat the Prime Minister of the United Kingdom quietly typing his speech with two fingers.

At that time the Labour Government was suffering under a tiny majority and soon afterwards Attlee dissolved Parliament and called a General Election. Morrison was on the high seas and from his messages it was clear that he disagreed with the decision. It is hard to believe that he was really enjoying his time as Foreign Secretary. More likely, he expected that Labour would lose and preferred that they should soldier on. But lose they did and he was out of office for life. We only saw him once again, when he dined with us in Bad Godesberg during an Anglo-German Königswinter Conference; he had lost his fire and seemed old and tired.

So Anthony Eden returned to the Foreign Office, obviously glad to be back. After Morrison, too, senior officials seemed glad to have an experienced and decisive Secretary of State again. But he was not always popular with those who worked for him. He was said to be unable to read a telegram without two officials at his elbows. One older colleague told me that Eden had once thrown a book at him. Another related how, at an Anglo-Russian encounter in the 1930s, Eden sounded off at him so viciously that Litvinov, of all people, leaned across the table and protested 'You are being unjust, Mr Eden.' I remember too that, when he came to Bonn on his triumphal tour in 1954 to rescue the German treaty after the French rejection of the European army, he was talking to the French and American High Commissioners. I was at his elbow in case of need, when he suddenly complained fiercely that our own High Commissioner, his host, was not supporting him. I was sent off to fetch him, rather surprised that my boss should be so sharply and publicly criticised to one of his subordinates before two foreigners. It has often been said that there was a touchy side to his character, reminiscent of what William Harcourt, speaking of Lord Rosebery, called 'pretty Fanny's way'.

Professionally too, as has again often been said, he seemed in some ways more suited to be a career diplomat than a politician, immersing himself in detail and not always seeing the wood for the trees. For example, it fell to me, when writing a paper in 1949 for the Permanent Under-Secretary's Committee, to look up Duff Cooper's famous despatch of 1944 from Algiers, fully described in his *Old Men Forget*, in which he pretty accurately foretold the course of events in Europe after the war. Eden had written a critical comment in red ink against almost every paragraph, but had failed to react to the main theme, which was that we could not expect Russian cooperation in the postwar settlement. Admittedly, all but one of our European heads of mission disagreed with Duff Cooper and looked forward at that time to a continuing alliance with Russia holding Germany in check, as was then the conventional wisdom. But a minister of Eden's experience might have been expected to take the wider view.

But I did not see enough of Eden in office to form a fair personal judgement, as we were sent abroad soon after the 1951 election. In due course Harold Macmillan succeeded him for a short spell at the Foreign Office. I did not see him in action then in London; but he came once to Bonn while we were there. He was in excellent form, even though he had never liked Germans much after his experiences in the First World War. Told that a wild pig had recently been shot on the steps of the Federal Parliament building, he remarked: 'I wonder how they distinguished it from the members.'

After we returned to London in 1958, I attended a good many meetings with Macmillan, by then Prime Minister, particularly over Cyprus, which was then the focus of much political controversy. His methods were very impressive. If one took a telegram for his approval he would go carefully and courteously through the draft, amending it line by line in his own hand. At policy meetings, too, he would start quietly discussing the paper before him, but would then suddenly raise the debate on to a higher plane, discoursing on the terrible human tragedy of the situation and so on, until one noticed that a stenographer behind him was taking down what was obviously his next speech to the House. But even then he could suddenly switch back to a more calculating level, showing that he was counting votes all the time and remarking in an aside that such and such an argument would not appeal to a few of his own backbenchers, but we need not worry about that because one of them was going mad anyway. The idealist and the cynic were nicely slotted together.

He had immense style and a sense both of fun and history. He laid down, for example, that all communications to the Russians should be 'prolix and obscure'. On one occasion, years later, I found myself next to him at a luncheon table. Searching for something to say, I remembered that I had recently read a statement by Isaiah Berlin that Churchill was one of the two greatest men of action whom the British nation had produced. I asked Macmillan who the other might be. 'Marlborough,' he replied at once. To keep the conversation going, I mentioned Cromwell. He then told me the story, which appears in Alistair Horne's first volume of his biography, how he had been with Churchill at the wartime Cairo conference with Roosevelt and others. Driving back from one meeting, Churchill had told him that Cromwell had been so obsessed with the power of Spain that he had not realised that the power of France was coming up behind. 'I knew at once', said Macmillan to me, 'what he meant: Roosevelt and his people were so concerned with Germany that they did not see that Russia was the threat of the future. So it can't be Cromwell; it must be Marlborough.' I have to add that, meeting

Isaiah Berlin soon afterwards, I asked him whom he had in mind. 'Cromwell, of course,' he replied. But at least Churchill was more prescient than Eden.

As Prime Minister, until the last year or so, Macmillan's touch seemed pretty sure. No one who has read the transcripts of his exchanges with Kennedy during the Cuban missile crisis can gainsay the skill with which he deployed a mixture of his avuncular relationship through the Cavendishes and his respect for a super-power head of state to influence the younger man's conduct of the affair. Again, during the Nassau meeting of 1962, after Skybolt had been snatched from our grasp, he emerged against all the odds with our independent deterrent preserved in the shape of Polaris. This was by no means welcome to some of the State Department paladins, who wanted to see Britain on a par with Germany as part of a European pillar of the Atlantic partnership, and without special relationships or privileges or independent nuclear weapons. But Macmillan was never one to be subservient to the Americans, despite his mother's nationality and his service with Eisenhower in North Africa. Nor, as a Tory in the Disraeli tradition, was he willing to see theoretical straitjackets imposed on political facts; the realities must generate their own conclusions. The Harvard professors were not to rule the roost from Foggy Bottom.

Above all in foreign affairs, Macmillan was a convinced European. If he had had more influence earlier, we might well have signed the Treaty of Rome at the beginning and shared in the exponential growth rate of the six original members of the European Community over the next ten years. We should also have been able to prevent the policies and institutions of the Community being organised for the benefit of some of its larger original members, in a way which we have come bitterly to regret and which has continued to cause friction and difficulty.

It is hard, contemplating the dominant figure of Macmillan as Prime Minister, to remember that he was once the naughty boy of the Conservative Party. During the war one of Chamberlain's former loyal supporters, whom Macmillan was later to sack from the Cabinet, said to me, recalling the Norway debate which led to Chamberlain's fall, 'And there was that nasty little Harold Macmillan mentally tossing himself off with glee.' Not many people would have spoken of him in those terms twenty years later. But the Conservative Party has a long memory and the establishment of the 1930s was to become the lower deck of the 1950s and 1960s, and vice versa. The resentment of the days of appeasement, and to a lesser extent of the Indian controversy, must have been the main blight on Rab Butler's later career; the prize pupil peaked too soon and then lost out to the former class rebels.

When we found ourselves in London again in 1958, Selwyn Lloyd had been Foreign Secretary for about two years. His reputation in that post has suffered from the Suez affair, in which he has been accused of suppressing the truth, if not worse. But, even if at that time and others he was unruly loyal to his Prime Minister, he was not a yes-man. He had a good lawyer's brain and always studied and mastered his brief conscientiously; he had a great capacity for taking pains. To his officials he behaved rather like a prosecuting counsel before a jury. His usual manner was a bluff and rather aggressive geniality. But this was generally a favourable omen. Only once, when I inadvertently gatecrashed a domestic occasion at his official flat, was he almost excruciatingly polite Then I knew that I had offended. In his single state he lived in almost Spartan simplicity, reminiscent of Lord Curzon who was reputed to have told a visitor 'You may be wondering at the austerity of my surroundings, but I can assure you that my wife's apartments are of unexampled magnificence.' Certainly when I had to take secret papers to Selwyn Lloyd in his bedroom the only place I could find to sit was on the end of his bed. But, despite his somewhat off-putting manner, he was tolerant and generous to those who worked for him. He must, incidentally, have been the last Foreign Secretary who came regularly to the office in a bowler hat.

With Lloyd too my main contacts were over Cyprus, which at the time was very much a party political football, more so than most matters of foreign policy. It was also to some extent a bone of contention between the Foreign Office, preoccupied with the reactions of Greece and Turkey, and the Colonial Office, and even more Hugh Foot, the Governor, who was impatient with diplomatic considerations and saw it exclusively as a question of the interests of the Cypriots themselves, including especially Archbishop Makarios, who was languishing in the Seychelles when I first became involved. These various factors had long proved irreconcilable, with EOKA terrorism continuing on the island and the Greeks and Turks slogging it out annually and inconclusively at the United Nations.

The breakthrough came from Zorlu, the Turkish Foreign Minister, and the only man I have sat next to at dinner who was subsequently hanged. Whatever his domestic deficiencies, however, he was a good ally and a constructive statesman. After the Greeks had raised the Cyprus question six times without success in the General Assembly, Zorlu approached Averoff, his Greek opposite number, and suggested that they should try to solve it by negotiation. So they repaired to a mountain-top near Zurich and soon brought down the tables of a new treaty to be endorsed by the colonial power in London, where there would then be a conference of Heads of Government, including Makarios, to sign it.

While we were examining this draft treaty clause by clause and had reached paragraph 51, a message was brought in to Lloyd, who glanced at it and looked at Zorlu: 'Foreign Minister, I am sorry to say that your Prime Minister's aircraft has crashed at Gatwick and we do not know if there are any survivors.' Zorlu, tough as nails, did not turn a hair but merely replied: 'Shall we go on to paragraph 52?' Luckily, however, Menderes had survived; he signed the treaty and on his return to Turkey was fêted by camels being sacrificed outside his front door – he had to wade through their blood to get to it. But he too was hanged within a year or two. Who said 'Scratch a Turk and you find a Tartar'?

After that, we had to negotiate the local details of the settlement with Makarios and the Turkish-Cypriot leader, Kutchuk. This meant a week of sessions in Selwyn Lloyd's room, to the exclusion of almost all other Foreign Office business. It cannot be often that an archiepiscopal crozier finds its way into that room. The Cypriots had conducted a campaign of violence for years in order to achieve freedom from British tutelage; but, when it was offered, they were not ready to accept it without a douceur of some £14 million as well. We wanted to keep our sovereign base areas, water supplies and the use of Nicosia airport; but this was the price we had to pay. Makarios was a tenacious antagonist and at least at one moment in the horse trading, Lloyd had to say to him, 'Archbishop, this is not worthy of you.' But the Archbishop, always spotlessly turned out, was a man of dignity and was quite ready to slap down his subordinates when they overplayed their hand. He knew when he had to settle and Selwyn Lloyd was a legal adversary who had his measure. We thought we had solved the Cyprus problem; how wrong we were.

As Chancellor of the Exchequer, Lloyd was later to be summarily sacked by Macmillan in the famous Night of the Long Knives, although he afterwards staged a triumphant recovery as Leader and then Speaker of the House of Commons. That night was imprinted on my memory as I was dining at Gray's Inn with my wife's uncle, Clarke MacDermott, who was a bencher. Lord Kilmuir was presiding in full finery as Lord Chancellor, lace ruffles and all, and did so with aplomb. When we opened our newspapers next morning we read that he had been dismissed. To this day I have no idea whether he already knew his fate or learned it later like the rest of us. If he already knew, he was almost as good an actor as his brother-in-law, Rex Harrison.

When Lloyd was moved to the Exchequer, he was succeeded by Lord Home, who was deservedly popular in the Foreign Office. He did not need or want the trappings of power. Indeed, as one of his private secretaries said, his office at any given time was the chair in which he happened to be sitting. Not only had he great charm, but the qualities of leadership as well. He gave us the advice, which, as he has related in his autobiography, his old cricket coach had given to him: 'It doesn't matter if you miss the ball, as long as you miss it in style.' As a stylist, too, he used to say that the besetting sin of Foreign Office draftsmen was the double negative. His status was such that Harold Macmillan accepted him as an equal and relations across Downing Street were more harmonious and more evenly balanced than at any time one can remember. But his modesty was genuine, too, as evidenced by his readiness in the tradition of Arthur Balfour, to return to the Foreign Office years after he had ceased to be Prime Minister. In that later reincarnation he stayed with us twice, in Tel Aviv and at The Hague, and one of our happiest memories is of watching him walk round our drawing-room pretending to be Harold Macmillan pretending to be far older than he really was.

During his first term as Foreign Secretary, he worked in double harness with Ted Heath, who held the office of Lord Privy Seal, although, as he used to say, not a lord, nor a privy, nor a seal. His special sphere of responsibility was, of course, the first abortive negotiations for our entry into the European Community, aborted quite simply by General de Gaulle. The first mention of Europe in history or mythology was when she was raped by a bull; while de Gaulle was President of France one could be forgiven for thinking that history was repeating itself. The Prime Minister gave Heath firm support and held more than one summit meeting with the General. A friend of mine who was interpreting on one such occasion said that Macmillan made a long speech and then went out of the room to check some papers, leaving my friend in solitary state addressing de Gaulle. This can hardly have appealed to the President, but in any case he was not to be moved into accepting British membership.

Ted Heath was never Foreign Secretary but his hour was to come later and it was certainly his finest hour, when, as Prime Minister, he eventually led Britain into the Community. He was a master of detail and it was said that to cover the details of the negotiations he took a rapid-reading course, with the result that when he read his statements to the House of Commons, they could not keep up with what he was saying. At small meetings in the Foreign Office, however, he was always a dominant personality, relaxed, humorous, the leader of his team. I was to remember this when, years later, he came to Holland to dine informally with the Royal Dutch Sailing Club. He stood up afterwards, hands in pockets, without a single note, and held them spellbound or rocking in the aisles with forty-five minutes of sailing stories. Even a landlubber lapped it up. Or again, later still, he came to preach at a service to inaugurate the newly restored organ at Chichester Cathedral, for which I had done some fund-raising; he gave a fascinating survey of the differences in liturgical use between British and Continental church organs, but, when I asked for a copy to study further, it transpired that he had spoken without any text. This certainly did not betoken lack of preparation; he has told me that he prepares speeches for days beforehand. As Winston Churchill said, 'an extemporary speech is not worth the paper it is written on'.

I did not see much of Ted Heath as Prime Minister. On one occasion I had to escort Aubrey Eban, Foreign Minister of Israel, on an official call. We had tea in the garden of No. 10, but Heath became so sharp in his criticism of Israeli foreign policy that I thought it best to invent another engagement for Eban and to break the party up. Another time I had to go and see him in the Cabinet Room. He greeted me rather gloomily from a sitting position and I said to myself that, before leaving the room, I would get him out of that chair. But it was not until I told him what a charming goddaughter he had, Olivia Seligman, who had stayed with us in Israel, that he broke into smiles and escorted me to the door.

When Home succeeded Macmillan at No. 10, Rab Butler came to the Foreign Office. If was the close of his long ministerial career and he was a tired, and no doubt disappointed, man, having had the prime ministerial cup twice dashed from his lips. He was only to hold the job for a year pending an election which he obviously did not expect to win, as was made clear in the famous interview which he gave to George Gale in a train shortly before the election took place. Several phrases in that interview were already familiar to those of us who had heard his observations in the office. He tended to be patronising about his chief: 'Alec is not doing badly, he is really doing quite well.' He himself was constantly looking for an initiative to take, but it had to be borne in on him that there were no initiatives for the taking just then. Even his visit to Gromyko in Russia, on which I accompanied him, was really aimed at the electorate at home and he took it pretty nonchalantly, announcing loudly to the chandeliers that he was sure they were not bugged and allowing himself to be sprayed with water in the gardens of Peterhof.

If he had no chance to be a great Foreign Secretary, he was certainly not a pompous one, but always friendly and informal. On becoming Foreign Secretary, he had some of us to sherry in his room, comparing it with the Home Office where he said he only met people whom the Permanent Secretary allowed him to see. As he drifted away, he murmured 'Keep in touch, keep in touch', as if one could drop in at any time for a chat. When one did see him, he certainly talked freely. Once he said to me: 'I thought of joining your profession, but then I married a rich wife and did not need to.' Another time, he told me, rather endearingly, that, as the Permanent Secretary was out, he needed my advice. I was a mere counsellor, with plenty of other hierarchs between him and me. Then he told me that the Prime Minister wanted to make a certain MP his Parliamentary Under-Secretary, and what did I think? I hope I was reasonably non-committal; the appointment was not made.

Whatever his stature as Foreign Secretary, Rab Butler was a splendid Master of Trinity, Cambridge, where our elder son was an undergraduate under him and where I must have sat next to him at dinner in hall at least three times. Once he bade me to stick close to him and I wondered why until I found on his other side a Russian political scientist intent on studying postwar Conservative politics, so that I was obviously a useful lightning-conductor for the more importunate questions and could also recount Rab's achievements in a way he was too modest to do himself.

Rab loved to be pressed to be indiscreet. He and Lady Butler made the Master's Lodge look lovelier than it had ever been, with the first drawing-room holding the college's Tudor and Georgian portraits, the second, since he had married two Courtauld wives, full of the Courtauld Impressionists and the third covered in cartoons of Rab himself, by such as David Low and Vicky.

A Labour Government came in after thirteen years of Conservative rule. Gordon-Walker was not with us long, as he was without a Commons seat and soon lost a by-election. As Foreign Secretary, he was saddled with some uncomfortable legacies from the party's election manifesto, particularly on the nuclear deterrent, which he was anxious to finesse. But he was perhaps still an Oxford don at heart; certainly, one seemed to spend a great deal of time in discursive seminars which did not meet the Aristotelian criterion of having a beginning, a middle and an end.

His successor, Michael Stewart, was deceptive. Sitting down, he seemed the quietest and most unobtrusive of men; when he stood up to make a speech, he dominated his audience. He usually had his way in Cabinet too. He used to say that his objective was progress by peaceful change and he practised what he preached. One of his stories has stuck in the memory: how, when he joined the Army in wartime, he went on his first day in uniform to the NAAFI for a cup of tea and, when the girl asked 'What do you want, soldier?', he looked over his shoulder for the soldier behind him. That story, suitably adapted, came in useful when one became an ambassador.

George Brown was a very different character. Many people in the Foreign Office disliked him. Some were plain frightened. He could be formidable and he had his prejudices. Once, when en route to Washington we were diverted to Boston airport in the middle of the night, with no one to receive us, he pulverised the unfortunate Consul-General when he eventually appeared, largely because there was no other target in sight for his wrath. But his bark was worse than his bite and the storms did not last long. He had a first-class brain which one could feel at work even when his speech was too slurred to be coherent. Secondly, he was genuinely interested in international affairs; and finally, he was determined to get things done and make them happen. For those qualities one could forgive him much.

Of course, his relations with his Prime Minister were appalling and he made no bones about it. If he started to dilate on the iniquities of 'him', one knew at once whom he meant. This was to be his downfall. On his last day in office, little as we knew it at the time, I was summoned to take the record of a meeting he was having with Bob

Bowie, formerly Counsellor of the State Department, head of the Policy Planning Staff and of the Harvard Center for International Affairs. After some exchanges on European unity, the talk turned to gold, which was then the flavour of the month. George Brown began to outline some of his ideas about gold and sterling, and there came a point when he said that 'Jim and I plan to put these ideas to Roy tonight'. Although Jenkins was now Chancellor of the Exchequer and neither Brown nor Callaghan had any direct responsibility for economic policy any more, Bob Bowie naturally pricked up his ears. But we managed to ride off a suggestion that the ideas should be telegraphed at once to the chairman of the Federal Reserve as if they were Government policy. The interview ended peaceably; but it was later that night, before George Brown had a chance to float his ideas, that he found that the Prime Minister and Chancellor were already at a Privy Council setting a two-tier price of gold. There have been many accounts of that night's events. Suffice it to say here that the Foreign Secretary resigned, not for the first time, but this time his resignation was accepted.

When he was no longer in office but still deputy leader of the party, he stayed with us in Israel. He came straight from seeing Nasser in Egypt and was trying to promote his own plan for Middle Eastern peace. Unluckily, the so-called war of attrition was going on and when we called on the head of the Air Force, Ezer Weizman, that afternoon, we learned that the Israelis had just bombed within five miles of Cairo. Obviously, this was not going to make the Brown peace plan any easier and the temperature rose. We were dining that night with the Foreign Minister, Aubrey Eban, who had planned an hour's tête-à-tête first, to dispose of controversial issues and then have a friendly dinner. I left them alone while I fetched Mrs Brown from her hotel; but when we came back it was clear that the stratagem had not worked. As soon as dinner started, George Brown left his allotted place and sat himself down in the middle of the table, from where he started to cross-question Vivian Herzog, an ex-general, later President of Israel and incidentally Eban's brother-in-law. It was 'General, why are you doing this bombing?' and 'General, do you expect to achieve settlement this way?' and so on for half an hour or more. I was sitting next to Herzog and when Brown paused for breath, I made some soothing remark to him to the effect that he had given the best answers he could. 'What did you say? What did the Ambassador say?' called Brown across the table.

It seemed best to stand up and break up the proceedings; George stormed round to tell me that my job was to support him. I started to demur, pointing out that he was no longer a Minister and I had to maintain relations with the Israelis. Luckily, at that point Sophie Brown came up and told him not to be beastly to me when I had looked after him on his trip. 'My wife says I am behaving badly. I shall go home.' We tried to dissuade him to no avail and I said I would drive him back. Unluckily, as we left the house we were met by a pro-Biafran demonstration who, when they saw him, started to chant 'Brown, go home', under the circumstances the least helpful thing they could have chosen to say. Once we were in the car, I expected to be roundly abused, but to my amazement George was full of remorse: 'Oh, I wish I didn't behave like this' and so on. I found myself acting the comforter rather than the culprit. Inevitably, someone from the dinner leaked the story and next day there were headlines, followed by telegrams from London asking what on earth was going on. George to his credit bore no grudges. But the best comment on the evening came the next time we dined at that house, with some of the same guests present, and Aubrey Eban, looking round the room, remarked: 'I see several veterans of the last supper.'

We kept a soft spot for George and for Sophie too. Once when I was staying at the Hassler in Rome, the Browns were in the same hotel and we were all bidden to dine with Pat Hancock at the Embassy. A quarter of an hour before we were due to leave, the reception clerk rang my room and announced: 'The Lord is waiting for you.' Feeling rather like the infant Samuel, I dashed downstairs to find George fuming because his appearance on Italian television had somehow gone wrong. I struggled to make soft conversation to turn away wrath while, after each of my gambits, Sophie muttered 'Change the subject.' Somehow, calm was restored and we had a relaxed evening. Another time, they were coming to lunch with us in Sussex on a Sunday, when nowhere could I find the wine-cellar key. Horrified at the thought of having nothing to offer George Brown to drink, my elder son and I charged the cellar door, at some damage to our shoulders, and brought up a few bottles. But in vain; when George arrived, he virtuously announced that he was on the wagon. I don't think he stayed on it long. At his memorial service at St Margaret's, Lord Shawcross said 'I used to tell him to stick to soda water and not too much of that.'

But it would be quite wrong just to remember George for his shortcomings. He was too big and too warm a personality for that and I remain his strong adherent. While he was a bit mixed up over the Middle East, having a Jewish wife and a pro-Arab policy, he was all through a convinced European and did a great deal to swing his party in the same direction. Not the least of his achievements, for example, was to appoint Christopher Soames to Paris in order to beard the General in his lair. In this and other ways he rose above mere party prejudice and I am sure that by the end of his life he had more friends than enemies.

When Labour returned to power in 1974, Callaghan was the new Foreign Secretary. Having been both Chancellor of the Exchequer and Home Secretary, he was a powerful figure in the party. But at first things were not very happy, least of all I suspect for him. Labour was committed to renegotiating our terms of entry into the European Community and it would be idle to pretend that there were many people in the Foreign Office who were enthusiastic about this policy. Not that the Foreign Office is a monolithic, conservative bloc, as many people outside it appear to believe. Like any other institution it is a collection of individuals, most of them intelligent and even more of them independent-minded. As William Strang used to say, the difference between the Diplomatic Service and the armed services of the Crown was that in the Diplomatic you could disagree with your superiors, always provided you gave reasons. Moreover, in those days, as Lord Carrington has noted in his memoirs, the majority of senior people in the Foreign Office probably voted Labour, while naturally carrying out the policy of the party in power. In my experience, there is in practice no such thing as a 'Foreign Office view'. So while in 1974 there was no opposition to the policy of renegotiation, as Mr Callaghan at first seemed to suspect, there were certainly misgivings among those of us who had to represent it in European capitals, when the struggles to enter the Community in the first place were still fresh in our minds. But in fact renegotiation passed off well and membership was successfully endorsed by a referendum. Any lingering thoughts of conflict between the Foreign Secretary and his officials faded away. When Lord Callaghan, as he now is, came to The Hague as Prime Minister two years later, he could not have been more agreeable. By then, of course, he had reached the top of the greasy pole and no longer had another occupant of No. 10 breathing down his neck. He himself was a formidable political operator; but as a man of Sussex after retirement he has continued to be excellent company.

Of his successor at the Foreign Office, Tony Crosland, I saw little. He stayed with us once at The Hague, when I chiefly remember a late-night session in our house with the then Irish Foreign Minister, Garret Fitzgerald, when I was kept busy as barman. Even then Crosland seemed to be subjecting himself to undue strain, although I suppose that this is an occupational hazard of the job. But I shall always be grateful to him for agreeing readily to recommend a peerage for a public man who had, I thought, been unfairly neglected and I was delighted to see it in the Honours List soon afterwards.

On Crosland's early death David Owen took over and was the last Foreign Secretary whom I served. He was reported not to be popular in the office. All I can say is that when he stayed with us as Minister of State before succeeding to the top job, he could not have been a more accommodating or less pompous guest, even sitting on the floor to dial his own telephone calls. His subsequent interventions in international affairs, notably at the time of the Falklands war, have also seemed to be wise and impressive.

Another very pleasant guest, who later became Foreign Secretary, was Peter Carrington. He came to The Hague as Defence Secretary soon after the Yom Kippur war in the Middle East, which had strained our relations with the Americans when we were reluctant to allow them staging rights for arms supplies to Israel or to risk an Arab oil boycott. Carrington was anxious to mend his fences and asked us to arrange a luncheon when he could talk informally to James Schlesinger, the US Secretary of Defense. It was not an entirely successful occasion: there was some tough talking and I remember at one time wondering whether the crockery was going to start flying across the table.

I have not mentioned two Prime Ministers who had never been Foreign Secretary: Harold Wilson and Margaret Thatcher. With Wilson I had little to do, apart from crossing the Atlantic once with him and Mrs Marcia Williams, on his way to visit President Lyndon B. Johnson. We were travelling in an RAF Comet, which could not cross the Atlantic in one hop, so that we had to stage at Gander in Newfoundland, where he was in relaxed form, reminiscing about the Cabinet discussions on Attlee's visit to Truman in 1950, in which I told him I had taken part. But when we arrived at Washington our journey had taken some seventeen hours and the Americans, used to a seven-hour crossing in a Boeing, were asking whether Wilson had stopped off at Moscow on the way, to brief himself for his talks with L. B. J.

Mrs Thatcher stayed with us twice: at Tel Aviv when Minister of Education and Science and at The Hague as Leader of the Opposition. Coming to Israel to open a British Agricultural Exhibition, she flung herself into a triumphant twenty-four hour visit with immense energy and enthusiasm. Not only did she tour every exhibit, leaving us with a photograph which I treasure of her riding high on a Lansing Bagnall fork-lift truck, but as a science graduate she fully held her own with Israel's leading nuclear scientist, Yuval Ne'eman, President of Tel Aviv University. With the expertise of her office she talked erudite shop to the Minister of Education and, sitting at luncheon next to the Minister of Agriculture, a gnarled old kibbutznik who had long since forgotten the joys of spring, she ended her speech by kissing him on both cheeks. Rarely does a visiting Minister enter so vigorously into the spirit of the occasion. At dinner we were able to introduce her to the then woman Prime Minister of Israel, Golda Meir, who said to me 'There is the first woman Prime Minister of England.' Mrs Thatcher was always supportive of Israel. When I said something to the effect that Judaism had for centuries been a religion of the underdog, she snapped back 'Not in my constituency it isn't.'

At The Hague she came to address the Anglo-Netherlands Chamber of Commerce. We gave a cocktail party for her and I stood at her elbow giving her a single-sentence steer on each incoming guest. She took her cues superbly and made each of them feel a million dollars for the next thirty seconds. The only people I have known do it so well were the Mountbattens.

We once met her at Hampton Court during Queen Beatrix' State Visit. It was just after the Bishop of Salisbury had published a book called *The Church and the Bomb*, attacking our nuclear deterrent. In what context I can no longer remember, I congratulated her on appointing Dr Leonard as Bishop of London, a staunch conservative figure. 'Yes', she said at once, 'but I appointed the Bishop of Salisbury too.'

Later we attended Tony Trafford's memorial service at St Margaret's, Westminster, where Mrs Thatcher read a lesson. It was the famous passage from I Corinthians about charity, which we did not think was quite her favourite subject. Nor was it easy to keep a straight face when she read the words 'when I became a man'.

Douglas Hurd became Foreign Secretary in 1989, and soon won golden opinions. It is perhaps lèse-majesté to remember that in the 1960s, when I went to see the Permanent Secretary in his room at the Foreign Office, the door used to be opened for me by a young private secretary called Hurd.

By now the worm's eye has started to blink and had better be shut.

6
London Life: Domestic Drudgery

Out of some thirty years working for the Foreign Office, I spent sixteen abroad and fourteen in London. Some people prefer working in London, either because they are at the centre of the spider's web and relish the feeling of giving orders to the outposts, or nowadays because they keep close to their families and their wives can carry on with their own careers, rather than going to cookie-push in unfamiliar and uncongenial climes. That was never my attitude. Admittedly, to begin with, in days of rigid exchange control, austerity, rationing and utility clothing England presented all the aspects of an economic concentration camp and the temptations to escape were strong. But, quite apart from that, one did not join the Foreign Service to live all one's life in London. London certainly had its attractions; but working long hours with telegrams arriving round the clock, hemmed in by the parliamentary timetable and always having to produce papers with never quite enough time to do so, one had precious little leisure left for restaurants, theatres and night-clubs, let alone the pleasures of family life, least of all when one's home base was in the country at the end of a commuter line. By contrast, abroad one had all the challenges of making new friends, seeing new sights and adapting to new environments, with one's own children around at least until they had to go home to boarding-school. Moreover, although Foreign Secretaries and other luminaries nowadays descend from the clouds like shooting stars, ambassadors and their minions can still exercise a modicum of judgement and take the occasional initiative. When abroad, one can express one's own views without having to penetrate so many ozone layers of hierarchy or negotiate compromises with so many conflicting interests. Although they had their exciting and even amusing moments, I do not look back on my years in the Foreign Office itself with any great nostalgia.

My first taste of it was depressing enough. Before going to Washington late in 1946, I spent a few days in the American

Department. The only piece of business which came my way concerned Magna Carta. One of the few original copies, I think from Lincoln Cathedral, had been sent for wartime safekeeping and exhibition to the Library of Congress in Washington. After the war the owners wanted it back, but the Library of Congress was not unnaturally keen to have another copy to put on show. The only copy still in private hands belonged to Miss Matilda Talbot of Lacock. Her Magna Carta was even then worth a million pounds; but she had no other assets and even had to write her letters to Mr Bevin on the back of her butcher's bills. Nevertheless, she agreed to present her priceless possession as a free gift to the Library of Congress, who of course asked her to come and hand it over in person. True to form, however, the Treasury refused to allow her dollars for the journey. Luckily, the United States administration came to her rescue; but the episode left a nasty aftertaste of 'candle-ends' parsimony and lack of imagination.

In 1948 I was summoned back to Whitehall and we started married life in London. We found a flat in Battersea, which someone said was on the wrong side of the river but the right side of the bank. Certainly our flat, with five rooms plus kitchen and bathroom, cost us less than three guineas a week. We also had Battersea Park as our front garden and, as during the Festival of Britain there was a long-lasting sculpture exhibition there of all the stars, Moore, Hepworth, Brancusi, Maillol and Co., we used to push the pram in the hope that some artistic appreciation would rub off. The drawback was Battersea Power Station: when we put the pram out on the balcony, it would come back in with the baby enveloped in smuts. In those days the straight route from Battersea to Westminster was by tram, which was all very well most of the time; but in those days we regularly worked on Saturday mornings and, if a friend was being married on a Saturday afternoon, I would find myself in glad rags of top hat and tailcoat next to a Nine Elms porter in full coal-carrying regalia. I was usually made to strip off my outer garments at the front door of the flat before being allowed to sully the sofas.

Meanwhile, in the office I had joined the Economic Relations Department, dealing mainly with commodity policy and non-governmental organisations in the supply field. This was the heyday of readjustment to the postwar economic situation and I spent long hours attending interdepartmental meetings on the supply and price of commodities from what came to be known as the Third World.

The protagonists were the Cabinet Office, Treasury, Board of Trade, Colonial Office and Ministry of Food. I never really knew what I was supposed to say on behalf of the Foreign Office. Not that my superiors cared much what I said or did. As far as I can see, many of the problems with which we were supposed to wrestle then are just as acute today.

Luckily, I was soon made the junior member of the two-man secretariat of the new Permanent Under-Secretary's Committee. This was an embryo planning staff, which had not until then been thought necessary, as the Foreign Office had hitherto worked on largely vertical ladders of authority, without much horizontal coordination between them. The work brought me into contact with Under-Secretaries far older than I was and no doubt antagonised most of my own contemporaries, who presumably thought quite rightly that they were directly responsible for the subjects in which we tried to interest ourselves.

The secretariat's main task was to draft policy papers, under the supervision of Gladwyn Jebb, for consideration by a group of Under-Secretaries, including the Parliamentary Under-Secretary, with the Permanent Under-Secretary in the chair. Hence the name. The most substantial paper we wrote was designed to show that Britain could not expect to build a third world force, able to hold its own with both the United States and the Soviet Union, but that, given the Stalinist challenge, Western consolidation was the only effective answer. It seems odd nowadays to think that in 1949 there could have been any doubt about this: it would have been much more open to question twenty or thirty years later when Europe had rebuilt her strength in unity and divergences had unhappily appeared between European and American interests. When we sought membership of the European Community, it was said that we were not trying to make the Channel narrower in order to make the Atlantic wider. But all too often that has been the effect. It is not just the Europeans' fault. From time to time both Americans and Europeans have acted without consulting each other and evoked the other partner's resentment, criticism and even divergent action. Obvious examples are American sanctions against Poland on one side and pipelines to Western Europe from Russia on the other. The need is for full consultation first and then a united front. But in 1949 all that lay far in the future. Our little secretariat's other achievements were much less significant: for example, we endorsed the principle that recognition of a state meant acceptance of its existence and not aproval of its government's policy and we laid down that the Eastern Mediterranean should be known as the Middle rather than the Near East. But with far more earth-shaking events engrossing the attention of the Under-Secretaries, the committee soon expired of inanition.

In due course this secretariat was transformed into a fully-fledged Permanent Under-Secretary's Department, with primary responsibility for liaison with the Ministry of Defence, so that, in theory at least, political and military planning could proceed hand-in-hand. I used to spend long hours with the Joint Planning Staff and occasional shorter sessions with the Chiefs of Staff themselves. The Chiefs then comprised Admiral Bruce Fraser, a true representative of the silent service, Field-Marshal Slim, mostly puffing on his pipe, and Air-Marshal Slessor, pouring out a stream of ideas mostly at variance with those he had lavished on us the day before. As it also fell to my lot to coordinate foreign policy briefs for what were not then called summit meetings and to write the Foreign Secretary's speeches, I was kept quite busy but also given a useful insight into the mysteries of policy-making.

All that came to an end early in 1952 and we did not find ourselves living in England again until the spring of 1958, when I was pitchforked into the Cyprus situation. That is to say, I was No. 2 in the Southern Department which dealt with a dozen or so territories along the northern shore of the Mediterranean, from Portugal to Turkey. But Cyprus was the political headache of the moment and luckily most of the rest of our region was quiet. Cyprus was a complicated problem. Our main concern was to try to reconcile the interests of Greece and Turkey not only with each other but also with those of the Governor of Cyprus, Hugh Foot, who was fairly impatient of diplomatic niceties, and his rear link in the Colonial Office. Terrorist atrocities by EOKA went on all the time. The essence of the problem was that the terrorism was designed to frighten us into accepting Enosis, the union of Cyprus with Greece, which was anathema to the Turks and not all that attractive to the mainland Greeks. It was not until all three participants showed themselves ready for an independent Cyprus that a window of opportunity appeared and even then we had to make it worth the Cypriots' while. What with non-stop telegrams from Ankara, Athens, New York and Nicosia and constant calls from the Greek and Turkish Embassies, not to mention endless parliamentary debates and questions, it was hard to satisfy anyone. Luckily we were dealing with two very civilised Ambassadors: Nuri Birgi of Turkey, later head of the Atlantic Treaty Association, and Georges Seferiades, otherwise known as Georges Seferis the poet and Nobel prize-winner, who had been Greek Minister with us in Beirut a few years earlier. Thanks to the Greek and Turkish Foreign Ministers, we eventually achieved a breakthrough with treaties which kept the peace for a time. One personal satisfaction in that settlement was managing to persuade the Government, against the advice of some powerful voices in Whitehall and others such as Archbishop Fisher, who talked about 'Makarios's blood-stained hands', to bring an independent Cyprus into the Commonwealth.

Hardly did we think we had 'settled' Cyprus than trouble broke out between Portugal and her African territories. Even some of our own Ministers, who would now be called 'wets', wanted to denounce Portugal and deprive her of all aid. We had to remind them that Portugal was our oldest ally and, while we could dissociate ourselves from her policies, we could not in decency denounce her, a fellow member of NATO. We had to make a fine distinction between arms which should be used for national self-defence in NATO and those which might be used for quelling internal revolts in colonies. There was also an episode where a rebel Portuguese naval captain hijacked a ship and sailed her across the Atlantic. We had to go through the motions of pursuing her and I had to tell the Vice-Chief of Naval Staff that we wanted him to try very hard to catch her but not to succeed. That is the sort of thing which gives diplomats a bad name.

The Portuguese connection did however earn me a luncheon for their Foreign Minister at Vintners' Hall; when my vis-à-vis sent away the wine because it was corked, I thought this a bold step even for a vintner, until I looked at his name-card and saw he was a VC, Brigadier Lorne Campbell.

The rest of our parish was less turbulent. The problem of Alto Adige, South Tyrol kept our Austrian and Italian clients nominally at loggerheads, but not disturbingly so. We witnessed the epoch-making election of Roncalli as Pope John XXIII but avoided raising our representation at the Holy See to Embassy rank. We made no progress in restoring relations with Albania; but we did settle the wartime claim of San Marino, on the macabre basis of paying £1,000 for each of the eighty citizens our bombs had killed. We kept in close touch with independent Communist Yugoslavia and indeed this earned me a trip on the inaugural flight by the Yugoslav airline JAT from London to Belgrade. The journey was preceded by a party the night before at the Yugoslav Embassy, where in some alarm we watched the pilots tanking up on slivovitz. As we took off next morning, the pre-breakfast aperitifs as offered were brandy, cherry brandy and, of course, slivovitz. So it went on for three days. Some of our Yugoslav Embassy colleagues were also on the flight; they came aboard with bowler hats, rolled umbrellas and stiff collars, to the London manner born, but gradually shed these capitalist appurtenances as they came nearer home.

So it was quite a variegated assignment. But I was not sorry when in 1961 I was sent on a sabbatical year to Harvard. It was a short respite; at the end of the academic year I was back for seven more lean London years as Head of Western Organisations Department, in effect dealing with NATO, Western European Union and the Council of Europe. (This appointment carried the incidental advantage of a room on the first floor bang opposite the front door of 10 Downing Street, where, through successive Governments, I would watch Ministers coming in and going out, in more senses than one.)

The Council of Europe was not much in the news. I usually attended the spring Ministerial meeting at Strasbourg, when the chestnut trees were proudly wearing their candles and the asparagus was at its juiciest. But the Council also carried out good if unspectacular work in concluding international agreements on practical problems. One such was on water usage and the signature ceremony was being addressed by M. Edgar Faure when the heavens opened and rain rattled deafeningly on the flat roof of our building. M. Faure took it in his stride and managed to raise his voice enough to declaim in favour of 'l'eau qui semble vouloir assister à notre cérémonie'.

There were memorable meals at Strasbourg too. Once we dined *à quatre* with Joseph Luns, the Dutch Foreign Minister, as one of the party. As a naval historian he started to enumerate Anglo-Dutch naval wars. He warmed to his subject and by the fish course there seemed to be more wars than had actually occurred. Luckily for Anglo-Dutch friendship someone changed the subject. Stories of Dr Luns abounded, mostly splendidly told by himself. One was of an official visit to Moscow as Foreign Minister. In his hotel bedroom was the usual chandelier reputed to have more functions than just shedding light. Luns, being immensely tall, addressed it loudly and distinctly on level terms: 'I hope Mr Gromyko knows how much I love caviar; I like caviar very much indeed.' When he left the airport for home, there was his opposite number Gromyko weighed down with a huge box of caviar. Looking down from his great height, Luns asked: 'Mr Gromyko how did you know?'

Western European Union took up rather more of my time, as its headquarters were in London and there were regular meetings of the Ambassadors of the seven member countries, where I sometimes had to deputise for Sammy Hood. But it was already rather an anachronism. It had been created for two main purposes: to maintain qualitative and quantitative controls on German armaments after the Federal Republic had joined NATO and to promote European cooperation in armament production. But by 1962 it was no longer practical politics to treat Germany as a second-class member of the alliance, beyond the restrictions which she willingly imposed on herself. Nor was there any British interest in doing so; although in the revised Brussels Treaty creating WEU we had undertaken to maintain forces of a certain size on the continent of Europe, we wanted from time to time to negotiate reductions in this commitment and it made little military sense to insist at the same time on arbitrary limitations on German forces. As for European armaments cooperation, this never really got off the ground. Quite apart from intra-European rivalries, where we British, unlike our Continental partners, usually at the time wanted equipment which would function as well east of Suez as on the European mainland, any pan-European project which did emerge was almost certain to be prevented or pre-empted by the powerful American defence lobby. All this involved a good deal of shadow-boxing.

But the discussions were not left to the Ambassadors alone. There were also regular meetings of the Foreign Ministers themselves, taking place in the member countries' capitals in rotation. The Ministers discussed not only the internal concerns of WEU but also their approach to current issues in world affairs generally. So these meetings required plenty of paperwork on briefs but we also vied with each other in finding pleasant places for official entertainment. We soon came to make friends among our opposite numbers and I remember some memorable meals.

Luckily, most of these opposite numbers were also concerned with NATO, which was a much more important and interesting preoccupation. Even so, seven years were too long to spend on one job. But it was certainly not a static period. We started with the Nassau Agreement, when the American abandonment of Skybolt suddenly deprived us of our main strategic weapon and Harold Macmillan with great skill persuaded President Kennedy to make Polaris available in its place on terms which preserved our independent nuclear deterrent. This was not popular with the theorists of the State Department, who did not want to see Britain occupying a more favourable place than Germany within the alliance. This led to the ill-fated multilateral force or MLF project, of which more anon. Then came General de Gaulle's withdrawal from the integrated military structure of NATO and the organisation's move from Paris to Brussels. Here our policy had to be that we should do nothing to drive France further apart from her allies: any distance between France and the rest of us should be of her making and not ours. Thus I believe we kept the way open for a return to closer cooperation later on. Finally we broke out into a new era when, with the Harmel doctrine, détente became equally as fashionable as defence and deterrence.

Perhaps these seven years are best described in art-historical terms. Between 1962 and 1969 NATO can be said to have gone through three stages: a constructivist period, with new designs held together by tenuous strings, of which the MLF was the prime example; a period of analytical cubism, when the apparent surface unity was broken up, mainly by the French defection; and a neo-realist period, with a deliberate search for new patterns, while the leaders of the alliance tried to put Humpty Dumpty together again. In 1969 it was strange to look back and reflect that in 1962 Harold Macmillan was Prime Minister, Adenauer was still Chancellor of Germany and Kruschev ruled Russia. Already it seemed like another world.

Incidentally, the politico-military picture of the world in the 1960s had a strange asymmetry: Britain looked mainly at the United States, the United States kept Germany in view, Germany principally focused on France, France mostly stared at Russia, while Russia kept its eye on China. China probably contemplated its own navel, properly Buddha-like. It was a multipolar world, rather like the film *La Ronde* of sexual liaisons coming full circle in old Vienna, except that in the 1960s none of the political love affairs was consummated.

It is also worth remembering that this period included 1968, the year of student unrest, known in France as 'les évènements'. There was nothing new in the younger generation disagreeing with their elders.

But heretofore this had been dismissed as misguided youthful ebullience, which would work itself out in time. Now for the first time people began to think that the young might possibly sometimes be right and that it could be worth listening to them. The dialogue thus begun has become a feature of our days and has not been unfruitful.

The MLF does not deserve to be forgotten entirely. The Nassau Agreement had envisaged a 'multilateral force'. While some Americans wanted to see British nuclear weapons subjected to multilateral control in such a force, the text of the agreement made plain that in the last resort we could use these weapons at our own discretion. Nevertheless, the American motives were not just anti-British; they genuinely wanted to find a role for Germany within the alliance, which would satisfy her national aspirations without giving her an independent finger on the nuclear trigger. So emerged the idea of a fleet of nuclear-armed merchant ships, each with a multinational crew. In the Foreign Office we were prepared to play along with this scheme for political reasons, partly to satisfy American critics of our independent deterrent and partly to show that we did not regard Germany as a second-class citizen within NATO. The Ministry of Defence, however, denounced the whole MLF as a military nonsense. They saw no need for yet another centre of nuclear command in the alliance. They were appalled by the problems of multilingual control both of navigation and weapons systems. Indeed, the Minister of Defence himself made fun of the prospect of the Turks celebrating Ramadan at the back end of the boat. There were others, including Lord Mountbatten, then Chief of the Defence Staff, with all his German ancestry, who were genuinely apprehensive of giving Germany even this amount of access to nuclear weapons. So, with American pressure upon us sustained, it fell to my lot to attend repeatedly on the Chiefs of Staff to argue the political merits of the case, while Mountbatten inveighed against it and threatened to give vent to his misgivings in the House of Lords. But I must say that he could not have been personally more charming: Admiral of the Fleet, belted earl, Knight of the Garter, he could easily have pulled rank and swept me aside like chaff. But when I apologised for taking up his time in argument, he would say 'Don't you worry: you are doing your job and I am doing mine.' I do not know how we should have resolved the conflict between the two Ministries across Whitehall, which often seemed more acute than the conflict across the Iron Curtain, had not the Germans become disillusioned with the whole business. When Chancellor Erhard told President Johnson that his government was no longer interested in the MLF, the Americans dropped it like a hot potato.

All this involved a great deal of travel, which atoned for the seven lean years. Not only were there the regular Ministerial meetings of WEU and NATO, in attendance on the Foreign Secretary. Occasionally I journeyed with the Prime Minister too. We travelled by RAF Comet One flight, with Denis Healey, then Minister of Defence but probably the best Foreign Secretary we never had, took us on the south-about route, having luncheon in the Azores, tea in Bermuda, both in glorious sunshine, and arrived for supper in Washington with the snow up to our knees.

Sometimes I had to go on my own and for a year or so was virtually commuting across the Atlantic once a month for two or three days at a time. Or I would fly with George Thomson, one of whose incongruous tasks as Chancellor of the Duchy of Lancaster was to negotiate the level of 'support costs', euphemism for the former 'occupation costs', for our forces in Germany. The Germans declined to pay them all and we needed to enlist the help of other allies. Thus we found ourselves one night dining at Blair House in Washington with the legendary Jack McCloy, Lord High Everything Else in successive American administrations, although he, like Benjamin Franklin, described himself as just a Philadelphia lawyer. He regaled us to a late hour with reminiscences of Roosevelt, Baruch and other giants of yesteryear, while we struggled to keep ourselves alert and him to the point. It was all very entertaining, especially when at breakfast he rang to say that he had already seen the President and secured us the money we wanted.

We went on to Ottawa where, after negotiating and lunching with Paul Martin, Minister of External Affairs and a Trinity man, whose name had the Canadian advantage of being pronounceable in either English or French, we were ushered into the Distinguished Strangers' Gallery of the Canadian House of Commons. Mr Diefenbaker, the Prime Minister, was making a portentously long speech when suddenly there was an almighty explosion. The press gallery emptied, but we thought we had to show British sang-froid and stayed put. We learned afterwards that a Quebec nationalist had strapped explosives round his chest, meaning to jump from our gallery into the chamber below, blowing us all sky-high in the process. Luckily in the last few minutes of his life he decided to go to the loo, where his bombs went off, harmlessly for us but fatally for him, in the smallest room in the house. I do not know why he could not have waited till the next world to relieve himself, but we were saved.

In these years I was also lucky enough to be a Foreign Office nominee to the new-born Institute of Strategic Studies, Alastair Buchan's brainchild. Strategic studies were not yet the growth industry which they later became. But they already attracted some formidable intellects, especially to the Institute's annual conferences, usually held in historic surroundings without any pain or discomfort. One found oneself in small smoke-filled rooms arguing with the likes of Dean Acheson or Helmut Schmidt. I am sure it all helped to cement the alliance.

Sometimes the NATO planners from the various Foreign Ministries travelled together in a bunch. On one such occasion we were ushered into the Oval Office at the White House to meet President Kennedy, who for some incongruous reason lectured us on the need for aid to Latin America. That time too we were introduced to Bobby Kennedy in the dark in Walt Rostow's garden; at close quarters he seemed much more impressive than his brother and perhaps his assassination was the greater loss. On another NATO jaunt, we were taken into the Strangelove atmosphere of the Pentagon control centre, with direct radio links to all independent American commanders around the world. The Chief of the Imperial General Staff was asked to whom he would like to speak and, when he named an acquaintance, some unfortunate general was woken from his beauty sleep in another time-zone, to exchange pleasantries at a moment's notice, obviously bewildered and none too pleased.

Somewhat surprisingly, NATO also brought me into touch with the Soviet Embassy. There was an exhibition at the V & A of English silver from the Kremlin, including a small tea-caddy very similar to one we possess. Wanting to check if theirs was by the same maker, Pierre Gillois, and about the same date, I asked the museum if I could compare them. But I was told that the Soviet Embassy had the keys and I must apply to them. This I duly did and was invited to call one morning when I found the caddy ready for my inspection. I identified it as Gillois whereupon the Russian diplomat who had received me said, 'You deal with NATO in the Foreign Office, don't you? I deal with NATO in this Embassy.' They do not miss a trick. This led to several questions and answer sessions over luncheon, until my contact was recalled to Moscow.

One uncovenanted bonus of my NATO connection was attendance at Winston Churchill's funeral. During the war he had prescribed exactly what the ceremonial should be and what foreigners should be invited. But meanwhile there had been a *renversement des alliances* and the numbers of seats allocated to each country were no longer entirely appropriate. Moreover, he died in January when many of his friends in the British establishment were away skiing or sunning themselves in warmer climes. So it became evident that there would be shamefully wide open spaces in St Paul's. The day before the ceremony members of the Foreign Office were told that we had to present ourselves at the cathedral next morning dressed in black. All my funeral garments were in the country, but I managed to beg, borrow or steal a scratch lot. Then I was told that I was to bearlead the Secretary-General of NATO, Manlio Brosio. This had the advantage that we had a huge black limousine to drive us to St Paul's. As a result, we arrived before the doors were open. Brosio said he wanted some coffee. Everything in the City was shut but, by asking a policeman, I discovered where a Lyons coffee-shop was open and led Brosio to it. He then said he did not like Lyons's coffee. I could have strangled him, but eventually found a basement café where, dressed as he was like a Christmas tree, he could drink coffee to his satisfaction. After that it was a relief to deliver him to his seat in the church and find my own in the south transept. The service was a most moving experience. For the first time there were television sets on every pillar and we could watch the procession coming all the way from Westminster in black and white and then emerging in full colour before our eyes in the Cathedral itself. When we sang the Battle Hymn of the Republic, we must all have had tears in our eyes. Two nights before I had queued for several very cold hours to witness the lying in state in Westminster Hall and had fortified myself with half a bottle of brandy, of which I felt that Winston would somehow not have disapproved.

My seven years in Western Organisations Department were made more agreeable by some excellent colleagues. Not only have many of them gone on to ambassadorial status, but they also included a future Vice-Chancellor of Sussex University, (Leslie Fielding) a future Deputy Private Secretary to the Queen, (Ken Scott) a future member of Labour's Shadow Cabinet (Bryan Gould) and a future head of an Oxford college (Mary Moore) – quite a good mixed bunch.

Perhaps the travelling highlights of those days were two trips to Russia, largely due to the kindness of Harold Caccia, the Permanent Under-Secretary, since East-West relations were only marginally my business as a Natonian. William Strang used to say that you could not understand Russia unless you had experienced it at first hand and I am glad to have had the chance to do so. The first journey was in 1963 for the signature of the Test Ban Treaty, which was also attended by three Foreign Ministers, the Secretary-General of the United Nations, half a dozen United States Senators and various other luminaries. At Sunday service in the Embassy drawing-room Lord Home read the lesson; and Ted Heath played the piano. Kruschev was in charge of the signature ceremonies, bouncing around with his round bald head like a little rubber ball and ideologically delighted when our Ambassador, Humphrey Trevelyan, introduced our legal adviser as a lineal descendant of Charles Darwin, even though Kruschev himself was most probably a Lamarckian believer in the inheritance of acquired characteristics. The entertainment was fabulous. We were regaled in parts of the Kremlin not open to tourists: the huge and glistening white St George's Hall and the domed rooms, walls covered in mosaics, in which the Tsars used to receive foreign ambassadors. Never in three days have I eaten or drunk so much. After one massive luncheon, Harold Caccia murmured to me 'We certainly shall not suffer from night-starvation tonight.' At that point, some double doors were opened to reveal tables groaning with sweetmeats, dessert and Armenian brandy.

The next year we went back for Rab Butler's official visit as Foreign Secretary, largely intended as an electoral gambit at home, without much international content. On both occasions the Russians were socially very genial, although in official meetings Gromyko was as unyielding as ever. Once we actually thought he had made some advance and I was sent to check with his deputy if this was so; Kuznetsov looked at me pityingly and said 'You can be quite sure Gromyko said nothing new.'

One day, at luncheon on the Lenin Hills, I was sitting next to Zorin, another deputy Foreign Minister, whom I had last known as the first Soviet Ambassador at Bonn. So we were speaking German when Semeonov, also a Deputy Foreign Minister of awesome reputation, leaned across the table and asked, in that language, why was I speaking German to Zorin. When I explained that we had known each other in

Bonn, he remarked 'Ah, among the aggressors.' This was becoming difficult; so I raised my glass and drank his health, whereupon he, still in German, abruptly asked if I collected pictures. When I replied that I sometimes bought a watercolour if I could afford it, he told me that he and all his friends in Moscow collected pictures, that he had a hunger for them and that whenever he travelled he first made straight for the local picture gallery. Despite this remarkable confession, he would not say what kind of pictures he collected. I doubted if they were socialist realism. Next day in Gromyko's office, when Rab Butler asked about one of the pictures, I suggested to Semeonov that he was the expert; the remark could not have had a frostier reception, made in Gromyko's presence.

Years later Semeonov was to shed his inhibitions and to emerge as a collector of avant-garde paintings, by artists such as Larionov, which he allowed to be exhibited abroad, and as an adviser to foreign collectors, who paid tribute to his help in Western glossy magazines, such as *Apollo*.

Shortly after Rab Butler's visit, I had organised a seminar at Oxford to discuss the future course of Soviet policy. It was attended by several eminent experts on Soviet affairs, who in the circumstances had better be nameless. They all with one accord spoke on the assumption that Kruschev would be in charge at the Kremlin for the indefinite foreseeable future. Michael Palliser and I diffidently suggested that we really did not and could not know what disputes and differences might be proceeding behind those hermetically sealed walls. We had hardly returned to London before Kruschev's demotion was announced. It happened on the same day that the explosion of China's first nuclear weapon was made known and I have always thought that there must be some connection. Had the politicians reached the conclusion that, if China was a nuclear power, the Sino-Soviet conflict was too dangerous to pursue and that it would be the path of discretion for Kruschev, as the protagonist of that conflict, to be discarded?

Some years later, in 1968, came the Prague spring. When the autumn reaction came, I was rung at 6 a.m. in the country on that Thursday morning to be told that the Russians had invaded Czechoslovakia. I managed to reach the Foreign Office for a meeting at half-past eight, still bleeding from a self-inflicted shaving wound, and we spent a busy day convoking the Security Council and so on. We could not do anything more effective on the spot and in fact the Russians had been careful to make overnight démarches in London and other NATO capitals to reassure us that they were only acting in their own backyard and not intending to pose any threat to the West. Be that as it may, it was ironic to go back to my office the next Monday morning to find the weekly intelligence summary advising us that the Russians would not be moving into Czechoslovakia.

All this was long before *glasnost*. In later years I have been back privately to Russia three times. In 1983 we took a tour round Soviet Central Asia: Tashkent, Samarkand, Bokhara, Baku, Tiflis, Yerevan. The ethnic problems were already raising their heads: while our local guides paid lip service to the government, it was clear that they were Uzbeks, Azerbaijanis, Georgians or Armenians first and foremost, and Soviet citizens only a long way behind. Certainly there was no love lost between them and our Muscovite Intourist guide. He was a remarkable young man, who had somehow missed his vocation of teaching history and had settled for working as a guide. This had the incidental advantage that he had a girl friend in every Intourist hotel. But when he and I, just the two of us, went to watch the Moscow Dynamos play the Tiflis Dynamos at the Tiflis stadium, he could no more read the Georgian language than I could; we found our seats by sign language.

That football match, by the way, was a revelation. It was played with three balls, so that when one went into the crowd, play at once continued with another; and in the half-time interval the front row of spectators turned and faced the rest of us, revealing themselves as soldiers with tommy-guns at the ready. No trouble on the terraces at Tiflis. But no bugging either and Boris and I could talk to each other in complete freedom.

Our young guide had no time for Western forms of democracy, remarking scornfully and truthfully that the President of the United States was normally supported by the votes of only a quarter of the electorate. The Soviet system, in his view, provided a stable government which worked to give the people what they wanted. But he was openly critical of the economy: 'The trouble about this country is that people do not work hard enough: they will only work if they have the incentives, the incentives they want are consumer goods and we do not produce the consumer goods they do want.' This was said in 1983, before any talk of *perestroika*, during the short regime of Andropov, although all pictures of Brezhnev seemed to have already disappeared almost overnight. But with an outspoken young man like this, *glasnost* was already casting its shadow before. Incidentally, when asked, in 1983, how long the Russians would be staying in Afghanistan, he replied 'About five years'; not such a bad forecast.

After another sightseeing tour of Moscow and Leningrad, where the restored palaces showed that the present rulers are just as imperial-minded as the Tsars, I went back in 1987 to travel with Jasper, my younger son, on the Trans-Siberian railway: three weeks from Liverpool Street station by train to Hong Kong, through Holland, Germany, Poland, Russia, Outer Mongolia and China. It was not the most comfortable journey in the world, but immensely intriguing. (We even rode a yak in the Gobi Desert.) What struck us most was the contrast betwee Russia and China, both professing and calling themselves communist. The Russians, even after two years of *glasnost* and *perestroika*, still looked pale and depressed, standing in endless queues, particularly outside the liquor shops which, under Gorbachev, did not open until 2 p.m., waiting for Big Brother to tell them what to do, whereas the Chinese were all bustling about on their bicycles, grinning from ear to ear and practising free enterprise on every street-corner pavement. We wondered if this reflected a difference of national character or just meant that Mr Deng had started his reforms earlier than Mr Gorbachev.

But this was of course before Tiananmen Square, which called into question the whole perspective of reform in China. It was also before the revolution of 1989 in Eastern Europe; never had I expected to live to see the Iron Curtain collapse and the Berlin Wall disintegrate. It was, moreover, before the tensions which we had observed in the fringe republics of the Soviet Union erupted into overt conflict and attempts at secession.

Winston Churchill said something to the effect that the Soviet Union was a riddle inside a mystery wrapped in an enigma. Never has that been more true than it is of the successor states today. Gorbachev sowed the wind and reaped the whirlwind. By advocating *glasnost* he unleashed the criticism which disrupted the system. Meanwhile the *perestroika* which he also advocated has not fully come about. Indeed one wonders how far the people really want it. Is there an entrepreneurial spirit to be fanned into action? Do the people want to make democractic choices or do they, as our young Intourist guide said, still prefer the smack of firm government capable of supplying their material needs from the cradle to the grave?

It remains to be seen whether a stable government can be maintained in Russia, let alone in the other successor states. Will there be a conservative backlash? Is the *nomenklatura* waiting in the wings ready to reimpose the dead hand of bureaucratic inertia and corruption? Will the influence of the defence establishment revive, even though historic Russia has no tradition of military coups? Will Russia itself dissolve further into its component parts? Or will it establish cooperative relationships with the other independent states within the so-called commonwealth? And what of Central Asia? It used to be said that by the year A.D. 2000 a third of the population of the former Soviet Union would be Muslim. If so, will Islamic fundamentalism create a new and assertive unity in that area? Will Teheran or Ankara or even Islamabad prove stronger poles of attraction than Moscow ever was?

But these idle and amateurish speculations bear little relevance to work in the Foreign Office between 1946 and 1969. As a mundane tailpiece, the practical discomforts of that work were legion. The building was totally unfunctional. Most of the lofty and well-proportioned rooms had been partitioned off into chimney-like cells. Intercommunication was by rattling tubes similar to those used in nineteenth-century drapers' shops. Coal fires had to be stoked by hand. There were no incidental services: if one wanted luncheon, or a haircut, or some medicine, or even a clean handkerchief, one had to walk to Trafalgar Square or across St James's Park. As I never served as an Under-Secretary on the inner ring of decision-makers, I had little chance to influence such things. But, if the powers-that-be had been prepared to let concessionary space to Marks & Spencer, Boots, W. H. Smith, Trusthouse Forte, a barber, and perhaps even Shell, they would have alleviated the lot and increased the efficiency of their officials as well as incidentally earning some revenue for the Exchequer to offset some of the Foreign Office vote. But perhaps the Security Service would have been too shocked.

7
Fitful Fifties: Beirut and Bonn

If the forties covered war, Washington and our wedding and the sixties mostly metropolitan monotony, we were abroad for almost all the fifties, with two years in Beirut and five in Bonn.

The Lebanon offered our first taste of the Middle East and we were not to go back there for fifteen years, when we went to Israel. Neither country is typical of the Middle East, in it but not of it; but once one has been in that part of the world it is hard to get it out of one's system.

With its confessional balance between the various Christian, Muslim and Druze sects, the Lebanon was of course unique. At the time we were there, these interlocking interests at least preserved a surface harmony, although later they were to erupt into all the horrors of civil war. Indeed in our day the country was still a playboy's paradise, almost a musical comedy. Later it was to become Wagnerian tragedy or, with its mixture of feudal chieftains and gang warfare, a cross between England during the Wars of the Roses and Chicago in the days of Al Capone.

For the leading politicians were not just representatives of their religious communities but local magnates as well, each with his territorial base and what the Russians would call his *khvost*, followers dependent on his patronage. These followers were not only his co-religionists but provided a private army for his bodyguard too. The Falange, which supported the Gemayel family, and which was to become notorious for the massacre of Palestinians in the Sabra and Chatila camps in 1982, was an extreme example. At a lower level of violence, a valuable element of each private army was understood to be a fleet of taxis, which were useful for conveying the leader's voters to the polls, for cordoning off his meetings against hostile intrusion and, in the last resort, if necessary running down his opponents. If anyone was involved in an accident with a taxi, it was no use seeking legal redress as the taxi-driver would be protected by his patron and the judge could well be in the patron's pocket too.

It is easy to be flippant and cynical about Lebanese political life. But one's heart bleeds too for a lovable people who have found themselves in the cockpit of forces beyond their control: Islamic fundamentalism, Syrian territorial ambitions, the Arab-Israeli conflict. They have moreover been at the crossroads of history, by land, by sea and latterly by air, for some 4,000 years. The inscriptions at the mouth of the Dog River testify to the forces which have passed through this narrow land, from Tiglath-Pileser to General Allenby and beyond. But the Lebanese were not just the victims of their history. They knew how to turn their position to their own advantage too, taking their percentage from all who passed through. The business of the Lebanon was business, and very good at it they were. This did not make for an egalitarian society. The divisions were horizontal as much as vertical and religious, with a handful of very rich, who bought their shirts in London and had them laundered in Paris, among a mass of very poor. Socially we probably only met 200 or so people outside the diplomatic corps.

The international tensions, too, were already operating. The refugee camps afforded a constant reminder of the Arab-Israeli dispute and of the reluctance of the Arab governments to absorb the Palestinian refugees, if that meant depriving themselves of a visible grievance against Israel. Syro-Lebanese relations were also always tense. The Syrians never gave up their dream of restoring the unity of the two countries which had existed under the French mandate. They maintained what amounted to a fifth column of Lebanese who also hankered after that unity. In these conditions there could be no diplomatic relations between Damascus and Beirut, so that driving into Syria one had to buy a visa at the frontier. The Lebanese civil war was eventually to give the Syrians their opportunity to intervene.

The Middle East, even if it does not always choose to recognise it, is a network of interdependent states. Jordan was another nearby country, though not contiguous with Lebanon. One morning I was sitting at my desk in Beirut when the telephone rang and a voice said 'We are sending an aircraft through Beirut this evening and want you to make sure that it is refuelled and sent on its way without any inspection of its contents or other delay or interference.' Recognising the familiar tones of our Ambassador in Amman, I said that I would do my best but that the Lebanon was after all an independent country and if I was to bully-rag the police and the customs, could he tell me a bit more? 'Oh yes, if you want to know, the King of Jordan has had a breakdown and we are shipping him out to a clinic in Lausanne.' He was referring to King Talal and that was how King Hussein, then a schoolboy at Harrow, succeeded to his father's throne. No one, calculating his chances then, would have given him three months on it, let alone thirty years or more. But just as he is a fine water-skier, leaning first on one leg and then on the other, so by a remarkable political balancing act he has kept himself in power all this time. He has proved himself an impressive survivor.

The King of Jordan was not the only casualty of those two turbulent years of 1952 and 1953 in the Middle East. The King of Egypt abdicated. The old King Ibn Saud of Saudi Arabia died. The President of Syria was dragged out of Damascus and shot. The Prime Minister of Iran, Mossadegh, was sent to jail. The first President of Israel died and her first Prime Minister resigned for the first time. The President of Lebanon itself was ousted in a midnight coup.

For good measure Stalin also died in 1953. Going as chargé d'affaires in deepest black to present condolences to the Soviet Ambassador, I started on a pompous speech of regret for our wartime ally. The Russian interrupted and with a cheerful grin told me to sit down and have a drink. He did not seem unduly to regret the tyrant's passing.

The coup which ousted Bechara el Khoury as President of Lebanon left a vacancy for which the candidates were Camille Chamoun and Hamid Frangieh, both of course Maronites. The Lebanese, who tended to believe that everything in the region was attributable to the nefarious intrigues of European secret services, were sure that Chamoun was the British candidate and Frangieh the French. The French themselves, with their residual suspicions of Lawrence of Arabia and 'l'Intelligence Service', did not entirely discourage this theory. Needless to say, we preserved scrupulous neutrality in the contest; but luckily for our prestige, Chamoun won. He had been Lebanese Minister at London and understood the British point of view, or at least the British way of life. For example, when a group of British politicians visited Lebanon, he invited them to dinner and after the meal asked the ladies to leave the room. This did not amuse Barbara Castle, who did not intend to be excluded from male chauvinist political gossip.

Even so, Chamoun was by no means always amenable to our wishes. In those days one of our main economic interests there was the pipeline and refinery of the Iraq Petroleum Company. The Lebanese maintained that, if the posted price of oil at Kirkuk was $x a barrel and its selling price at the Mediterranean port of Tripoli was $y, where y was much larger than x, then it had acquired a substantial added value of $y–x as a result of its passage through Lebanon, on which the Lebanese were entitled to charge a tax. In vain, as chargé d'affaires for the best part of six months, did I argue with Chamoun week in and week out that we had long since paid way-leave for the pipeline and that the Lebanese had contributed nothing which could justify them sharing in the profits. Chamoun was not to be moved. Not for nothing had the Lebanese for centuries been at the meeting-place of the camel-routes and the sea-lanes. The issue remained unresolved.

In view of the miseries which Lebanon has later endured, it may seem heartless to recall the lighter side of life there then. We had hardly arrived in the country, for example, only a week after King George VI had died, when we were bidden, dressed from head to foot in black, to luncheon with the Speaker of the Parliament in his mountain fastness in Southern Lebanon. He was the Shia feudal chieftain of the South. As we drove towards his castle, I asked the name of an attractive white flower growing beside the road. Surprised that I should ask, our guide said it was hashish. 'But surely hashish is illegal?' 'Yes, of course, but Parliament has passed a law forbidding its growth. This sends up the price and, when enough has been grown on the Speaker's land, he will have the law repealed and his crop will be sold at the top of the market.'

Sometimes one could invoke the law to our own advantage. One day the local Communist paper published a picture of Princess Margaret attending Lord Dalkeith's wedding, with a caption meant to say that she was looking very gloomy. That was innuendo enough. But, thanks to a misplaced Arabic apostrophe, the caption actually read 'looking very pregnant'. This was too good to miss. I drove down, all flags flying, to see the Foreign Minister and demand condign punishment for the Communist rag. He entered into the spirit of the thing and hardly was I back in the Embassy before the editor appeared, profuse in abject apologies, protesting his undying devotion even as a Communist to the British Royal Family and begging that we should forgive him and above all not cancel our meagre subscription to advertisements in his newspaper.

Even more devoted to the Crown were the rulers of the Gulf states, then still British-protected persons. When one of them, aged about sixty-five, arrived one day for unspecified medical treatment, I paid my formal call, mouthing polite platitudes about 'the Queen, my mistress' and hoping this did not sound like lèse-majesté. The entertainment consisted of a Nubian slave handing the sheikh a cup of coffee and then, without wiping it, refilling it and handing it to me. Not knowing for what disease he was being treated, I feared the worst, went home and washed myself from head to foot. After cautious enquiries I later found that he wanted his masculine powers revived and was so pleased with the result that on returning home he sent his uncle, aged ninety, for the same rejuvenation.

King Saud of Saudi Arabia was more alarming. When he came on a State visit and the diplomatic corps were paraded past him, he was flanked by two huge Nubians, each holding a vast scimitar. It was uncomfortably reminiscent of the Mikado and his snickersnee and I made my bow from a discreet distance.

One of the pleasanter aspects of life at Beirut was the number of British naval visits, notably from Lord Mountbatten, then C-in-C, Mediterranean. Once he brought his whole family in his despatch vessel, HMS *Surprise*. It was an education to see not only his professionalism and Lady Mountbatten's charm and energy at close quarters, but also the viceregal skills with which they at once made friends of everyone introduced to them. The wardroom in *Surprise* was tiny: after dinner, although the Commander-in-Chief cannot have had a drop of Scottish blood in his veins, he had two pipers playing round the table in that confined space. Banshees were not in it.

Another time he came to my rescue when the SS *Champollion* of the Messageries Maritimes ran aground just off Beirut's most fashionable bathing beach. There were scurrilous stories about the reason why. But there the ship was, her back broken, a hundred yards from the shore, in a raging sea. The first I knew of it was late at night, when the Military Attaché appeared beside my bed to tell me. I asked what he expected me to do and he said 'You could always send for a cruiser.' In my bemused state I indicted a telegram to the C-in-C, Med and went back to sleep. The next I knew, it was early morning and there was the Military Attaché at my bedside again, reporting to my dismay that the cruiser had arrived. So we had quite an active day trying from the beach to direct the cruiser's operations so as to help the stricken ship. President Chamoun and most of the *beau monde* turned out to watch. But it was far from entertaining and came near to being a Roman holiday. At one point the captain seemed to have lost his nerve and given the order 'Sauve qui peut', so that seventy passengers launched themselves into the waves, of whom only some fifty reached the shore alive. The rest were being drowned before our eyes. Luckily the other passengers did not panic and it was by a remarkable feat of seamanship that the local harbour pilot managed to slip his boat round the *Champollion's* bows and disembark the survivors from the leeside. In the end we could not do much to help as our cruiser could not come close enough inshore.

The wife of a French colleague had been aboard the ill-fated ship. When her time came to climb over the side, she remembered that her husband had always told her in a shipwreck to tie her jewels round her waist. She duly did so but forgot that, being eight months pregnant she had no waist as such. The jewels slipped off her and were lost in the sea.

Unusually for an Arab country, women played a prominent part not only in social life but in commercial activity as well. One of the loveliest of them all, who was as astute as she was beautiful, had an aged mother who was unwise enough to die in Damascus, although the family burial-ground was in Beirut. The Lebanese propensity to impose import duties applies even to dead bodies. So this dutiful and beautiful daughter, who had no intention of paying the tax, propped her mother up in the back of the car and, as they approached the frontier, lit a cigarette, placed it between her mother's lips and drove across, duty-free.

But things were not usually so macabre. Most of the time we lived a life of lotus-eaters. Our home was a flat on the Rue el-Hamra, where we could sit on the balcony and watch an endless procession of camels, cadillacs, fattened turkeys and performing bears, the medieval and the modern mixed. There were times of year when one could ski near the cedars of Lebanon in the morning and swim in the Mediterranean in the afternoon. In the heat of summer, before air-conditioning took over, we retreated to hill-stations for three months, beautifully cool for our families, even if the unfortunate breadwinner had to descend into a new hell every morning. We ourselves rented a villa in Shemlan village, then home to the British Centre for Arabic Studies. The main subject of local gossip was to determine which student's wife the Druze sheikh of the neighbourhood would set out to seduce that year. By all accounts he usually succeeded.

Even so, there were drawbacks to this Elysian existence. During the two years we were there, not a baby was born and lived in our Embassy. Whatever the causes, and no doubt they were various, this inevitably led to strain. Then, hard as it is to believe after all the trials and tribulations through which unhappy Lebanon has later passed, the actual diplomatic work at the time was pretty dull and uneventful, although, as Head of Chancery in charge of discipline, I remember one morning when I had to deal with three British officials, one a suspected homosexual, one accused of spying and one for allegedly passing dud cheques. Meanwhile, news from home was bad: my father, after nearly thirty years as Bishop of Birmingham, had had to retire through bad health and was obviously very ill. We had had to join in buying, sight unseen, a house for his retirement. So for the only time in my life I asked to be transferred nearer home and have always been grateful that I was able to spend a last week with my father between Beirut and Bonn. He died within a few days of our arrival in Germany.

Bonn was of course totally different from Beirut. It used once to be said that, while the situation in Berlin was serious but not grave, the situation in Vienna was grave but never serious. Certainly, in the 1950s Beirut was neither grave nor serious. In Bonn life was much more serious but luckily not grave.

No Englishman of my generation, who was born in one world war and served in another, can be indifferent to Anglo-German relations. There were family factors too. My grandfather had been brought up in Germany where his father had been in various diplomatic posts, before in fact there was a Germany, except as a geographical expression. He always wrote to his brothers in German: one of them had married a German wife and the other ended his career as Consul-General at Hamburg. My grandfather too spent much of his long life writing about German history and his written style was itself regarded as ponderously German. He was in touch with many German scholars. So our family was predisposed to Anglo-German friendship and this tendency was reinforced by my father's pacifism, which led him to dislike the Treaty of Versailles and to try to build bridges to our former enemies. He was, for example, one of quite a small group who attended the first reception given by the new post-war German Ambassador in the early 1920s. This did not reconcile him to Nazi methods when they came along; but it did make him all the keener to see another war with Germany avoided.

I myself did not go to Germany until 1936. Having spent several holidays in France learning French, it was now time to improve my German, which had not made much progress at Winchester, which was not all that surprising as I was taught it there by a Frenchman. On a Greek cruise we had met Elisabeth Dabelstein, a strong anti-Nazi who found a sea-trip of that kind the only way of escaping for a short time from the Thousand-Year Reich. With a Dutch and a Danish colleague, she kept a *Jugendheim* at Oberstdorf in the Bavarian Alps and there I went for my first German stint. It meant travelling all the way, for thirty-six hours or so, third-class on wooden benches. But when one arrived, it was a lovely place, where one could walk in the mountains, swim in the lakes or just breathe the air which seemed to taste of milk. I was also given fairly systematic instruction in the German language and German manners, both badly needed.

After some weeks of this I moved to Munich as a paying-guest of Frau Meier-Graefe, whose husband, although I did not appreciate it at the time had been one of the first art critics to welcome post-impressionism. He would not have been popular with the Nazis, whose exhibition of Degenerate Art was then showing in Munich, full of derided works by modern masters which would nowadays sell for millions. Helene Meier-Graefe was not as outspokenly anti-Nazi as Frau Dabelstein, but her sympathies were clearly with non-conformist liberals and artists. One of her friends was Gusti Oesterreicher, the pioneer graphologist, who in that same year of 1936, in response to the wife of Stanley Baldwin's parliamentary private secretary, had passed some scathing comments on Mrs Simpson's handwriting. Another, who took us for drives all over the countryside, was Christa Winslow, author of *Mädchen in Uniform* and in private life a Hungarian baroness and thus not subject to Nazi discipline; she was to die tragically, working for the Resistance during the war, shot in error by her own people. When I went back to Munich in 1945, I tried through the official record office to find some trace of the Meier-Graefes, mother and son, but without success.

The next year I enlisted in holiday courses for foreigners at the Universities of Freiburg and Marburg, staying with families in each case. In Freiburg the Sohlers, though looking impeccably Aryan, turned out to have a Jewish grandmother. We were able to help Erika, their daughter, to come to England, where she started as a nurse at the Queen Elizabeth Hospital at Birmingham and later married William (Bo) Mann, for long music critic of *The Times*, with Budge Firth, his Winchester housemaster, officiating and my mother giving Erika away. At Marburg I stayed with Professor and Frau Deutschbein, whose name seemed fairly obviously to mean 'German leg', but they insisted that it signified 'friend of the people'. Crossman had been one of their earlier English visitors and, as might be expected, had made a powerful impression on the household. Nonetheless, the Deutschbeins were not noticeably hostile to the régime; at least one senior officer of the Reichsarbeitsdienst dined in the house in uniform. But they were not aggressively partisan either and I had the impression that in the academic world a measure of dissent was still tolerated. With hindsight I imagine that most of the people I met were consciously keeping their heads down. They were aware of concentration camps and the régime's hostility to the Jews; they knew that the party was all-powerful and that it was imposing economic austerity for the sake of nationalist ambitions. But they would make little jokes about their new leaders and would maintain that, whatever the current drawbacks, they were better off than under Communism. When one protested that they had never known Communism, they quoted the inflation from which they had suffered after the First War and which they attributed to Communism. The fear of inflation has remained dominant in German minds ever since. They also seemed genuinely to believe that Germany was surrounded by hostile forces which it was incumbent on her to resist, although they politely did not apply this to the English visitor in their midst.

Such was my brief, trivial and superficial experience of Germany before 1939. I was next there, in uniform, for a few months in 1945–6, as one of the conquering hordes. But then we lived in an entirely Allied world, more or less insulated from the German economy. The only German with whom I remember having dealings was Herr Krupp's estate carpenter, who made me a splendid cedarwood chest, which has stored linen round the world for nearly half a century. It cost me twenty cigarettes.

The effects of the war were everywhere apparent. But already one could sense the determination of the German people to rebuild their country and one knew that they were well supplied with the natural resources with which to do so. At that stage there were no politics and thus no general direction of society, except what the occupying powers provided, and that was largely limited to the prevention of disease and unrest. It was more a matter of individual self-help, with the initiative coming from the grassroots.

So, when we went back in 1953, it was to a very different Germany.

In the infant Federal Republic both politics and economics had made a vigorous rebirth. Admittedly, it was slightly alarming to be confronted at the border by those hard, high-peaked caps of customs officers, which one remembered so well from the 1930s. But this was in fact a self-consciously but genuinely democratic Germany, more interested in forgetting than remembering the past. But it was also a Germany conscious of its economic strength and already determined to regain a position in the political big league, without at the same time attracting odium by any excessive self-assertiveness.

The architects of this new Germany were the old firm of Adenauer and Erhard. It was not an equal partnership. As Chancellor, Adenauer was very much the senior partner and determined to remain so. But it was Erhard who underpinned him, who had presided over the successful currency reform and set in train the Wirtschaftswunder which was in full swing by the time of our arrival.

In theory the Federal Republic was still governed by the High Commissioners, representatives of the three victorious Western powers. But this constitutional nicety was already more apparent than real. The significant change had occurred when Adenauer, having for long daily ascended the Petersberg mountain to receive the tablets of the law from the High Commissioners, had succeeded in reversing the position and forcing the Mohammedan trinity to descend from their mountain to confer with him. It was an achievement comparable with that of Talleyrand, who had also, after the Napoleonic Wars, turned defeat into victory and divided and ruled his conquerors. 'Graecia capta ferum victorem cepit.'

In his own Government too Adenauer kept the reins of power firmly in his own hands. In 1953 and for some time afterwards he was his own Foreign Minister. There was a Foreign Ministry, it is true, but we hardly ever dealt with it. It lived in a twilight zone down the road. The powerhouse of German diplomacy was the Federal Chancellery in the Palais Schaumburg, where, under Adenauer, Hallstein and Blankenhorn, disrespectfully known to us as Rosencrantz and Guildenstern, were articulating Germany's voice in Europe and the world.

In fact, the terms of our work were largely set by what was known of Adenauer's interests and prejudices. There was not at that time much talk of European unity. but Franco-German friendship was known to rank high among his priorities and he attached importance to his links with Robert Schuman, father of the Coal and Steel Community, and also with Alcide de Gasperi of Italy. All three men were Catholics by politics and conviction and all three incidentally had served in armies fighting against the Allies in the First World War. In this context Adenauer's main aim was to integrate Germany firmly into the Western world. He set the tone for his successors.

Reunification remained a stated aim of his policy which had to be reaffirmed at every turn. This was not just lip-service. But he obviously did not regard it as immediately practical politics. It was more in the nature of a sacred cow. Indeed he showed little interest in negotiation with the Russians at all and was suspicious of Winston Churchill's hankering after an accommodation at the summit or of non-agression pacts and the like. His attitude seemed to be that in due time the weaknesses in the Soviet position would show themselves and then the West could exploit them without going begging first. In those days he made a book by Starlinger, *Grenzen der Sovjetmacht*, required reading for his followers and therefore for us diplomats too. The thesis of the book, written by a former inmate or *zek* of Vorkuta concentration camp in northern Siberia, lay in its title: the limits of Soviet power. The *zeks*, having no prospects for the future and therefore nothing more to lose, had discussed freely the weaknesses of the Soviet system, containing within itself the seeds of its own decay. This encouraged Adenauer to play a waiting game.

But even he could not fail to respond to the Russians when in 1955 they offered to return the German prisoners of war in the Soviet Union in return for the establishment of diplomatic relations between Bonn and Moscow. A refusal would have been electorally impossible, quite apart from the opportunity to relieve much human misery after ten years or more of captivity. He did not relish carousing in vodka at the Kremlin when he would have been happier drinking his beloved Rhine wine at home. But he went to Moscow and concluded the agreement. When the prisoners came back, there were some tragic problems. One man was brought to see us who had spent all those years as a prisoner, cut off from the world, but sustained by the hope of seeing his wife again. Now he came back to find that she had at last presumed him dead, married again and had more children. Who could blame her? But whose wife was she? The dilemma was total. How can one solve a human problem of those dimensions, and there must have been many such cases. But there must have been many happy endings too.

What really mattered to Adenauer was power, international and domestic. Internationally he was determined to regain German sovereignty and this he achieved in 1955, together with German membership of NATO, after the crisis following the French rejection of the plan for a European army. We had some hectic times renegotiating the treaties to put these arrangements into effect and burning much midnight oil in the process. The climax was the Paris Conference with Adenauer, Dulles, Eden and Mendès-France sitting round quite a small table to hammer out the final details. One could see that Mendès-France was a red rag to Adenauer's bull; Dulles and Eden had to keep the peace between them. But in the end General Ismay was able to lead Adenauer triumphantly into the North Atlantic Council as a full and equal member. After that achievement, Adenauer actually agreed to relinquish the Foreign Ministry to a separate Minister, Heinrich von Brentano.

Internally, his main aims were to keep the Social Democrats, whom he profoundly mistrusted as unpatriotic, out of power and to maintain his personal ascendancy in his own Government. Every Christmas and New Year he used to retreat to the warmer climate of Italy. While the cat was away, the mice used to play and he usually on his return found himself having to restore order among his Ministers. On one such occasion, when he was already over eighty, I drafted a report to London saying that the old man was busy exhibiting his vigour. Unluckily my handwriting resulted in the word 'vigour' being transmitted as 'organ'. 'The Chancellor is busy exhibiting his organ.' I was nearly sacked.

This is not meant to be a history of post-war Germany. But it does perhaps show how one man imprinted his personality on his country during his term of office and, more importantly, how many of his plans and expectations have proved right in the long run, some of them after his departure from the scene. He was truly *pater patriae*. He would not have welcomed the comparison, but he set the tone for the new Germany very much as Ben Gurion did for the young Israel.

The work of the Chancery was pretty heavy, reporting on the political scene, reaching agreement with our French and American allies, determining policy on Berlin and ensuring access to it, establishing relations of confidence with the Chancellor's office and later with the Foreign Ministry, preserving contacts with British forces in the Federal Republic and so on. But it was not all work and no play. Bonn was an excellent place to get away from. That is not meant to be rude to the capital of the Federal Republic. But there we were, bang in the middle of Western Europe, and in five or six hours we could be in Munich, Berlin, Paris, Brussels or Amsterdam. Many of our weekends were spent ingesting the fruits of Bavarian rococo, the Dutch golden age or Parisian cuisine.

But Bonn itself had plenty to offer too. We lived in Bad Godesberg, John Le Carré's 'Small Town in Germany,' in one of a row of houses built from 'occupation costs' in an apple orchard, so that one had the illusion, unusual for a European capital, of living in the country. Official entertaining was active and constant, so that in five years we collected a wide circle of friends, official, diplomatic, journalistic and private.

Some German officials, let us face it, were unreconstructed opportunists, who would serve any régime. It became rather wearying when one's neighbour at dinner started the conversation with 'Mein Mann war nie Nazi'. Methinks the ladies did protest to much. But it was encouraging to hear a dinner-jacketed guest at one's dinner table saying that, two years before, his entire worldly possessions had been in two suitcases which he carried across the interzonal frontiers. Others were truly representative of the new, reformed Germany, if that does not sound too patronising. One such was Fritz Caspari, who became godfather to one of our daughters and has remained a firm and dear friend. When Hitler came to power in 1933, he was a Rhodes Scholar at Oxford and his father telephoned to warn him not to come back to Germany under the Nazis. So he went to the United States and after many vicissitudes, including internment as an enemy alien, he became a full professor at Chicago, specialising in the sixteenth-century humanists, and married an American wife. There he could have stayed, prosperous and respected; but, when the German Foreign Service was reconstituted, he decided that it needed people not connected with the Nazi régime and returned to Bonn to start at the bottom as a humble Second Secretary in the Foreign Ministry, where, to our great good fortune, he was in charge of the 'British desk'. He rose to be diplomatic adviser to a very liberal Federal President, Gustav Heinemann.

Anglo-German relations were also sustained by the Deutsche-Englische Gesellschaft and its annual Königswinter Conference, which brought us the opportunity to meet and entertain a number of English people, some of them old friends, many already distinguished and others who would achieve distinction. One of the best was Hugh Gaitskell, by now shadow Chancellor of the Exchequer. But we knew him far more as a human being than a political figure, and very human he was too, always with an ear for the latest dance tune and an eye for the prettiest girl within range. The greatest loss to British public life of our generation.

There were plenty of other foreign visitors to Bonn, most of them anxious to make their number with the renascent Germany. One State visitor was President Tubman of Liberia. He found the ceremonial pretty stuff and, after dinner, turned to his ADC and told him to fetch his medicine from his bedside table upstairs. After a prolonged interval, the young officer reappeared, bearing a bottle of Scotch. Tubman turned on him in fury: 'Surely you know my medicine has to be wrapped in brown paper.'

Two of our children were born in Bonn, in a maternity hospital appropriately situated on the Venusberg. The two older ones attended the junior French *lycée* at Bad Godesberg. The education was excellent, but it was interesting to find that all the battles which the English had won when I was at school had either been won by the French or had apparently not taken place at all. The children also had their first taste of skiing at Wintersberg, the British army leave centre in the Sauerland. I only remember our elder son, then aged about six, proudly announcing that he had come second in a ski-race; when we asked how many competitors there were, the answer was 'two'. We took them once to Wiesbaden to see the famous head of Nefertiti, who was still exiled there for safety from Berlin. As we were leaving the museum we came on a most lifelike tapestry depicting Leda and the Swan. Our eldest daughter, four years old, showed precocious interest, put her finger on the focal point of the picture and asked 'Mummy, what is this bird doing?' Before my wife could frame a suitably bowdlerised answer, an attendant descended on us in full cry for touching the exhibits: 'Du schreckliches Kind, was tust Du da? und so weiter und so weiter.' Our daughter set up a howl of anguish and we left the museum in disgrace and disorder. I do not think that attendant was representative of the new and gentler Germany.

8
Interest in Israel

Obviously, wherever it is, one's first independent diplomatic post is an exciting assignment. But there was special excitement in going to Israel, to a country unique in so many ways. By definition the only Jewish state in the world, Israel is a partner in no alliance and a member of no economic community. It is in the Middle East but not of it, a country of largely European origin, hanging on the rim of the continent of Asia. It is probably the only member of the United Nations, except South Africa, which cannot hope in existing circumstances to be elected to the Security Council. It is, incidentally, reported to be the site of the first recorded city, at Jericho, the first recorded farm, at Degania, and the first recorded battle, at Megiddo or Armageddon, in all human history.

But for me personally, appointment to Israel also called for some adaptation. I knew little of Jewry or Judaism. My father had been vaguely anti-semitic. I am not sure why. He can never have had many Jewish acquaintances. His prejudices were those of many of his generation: partly religious, partly national and partly, I suppose, social. His Christianity took a puritan form belonging far more to the New Testament than to the Old. While he would not have endorsed the crude accusation that 'the Jews killed Christ', he would probably have thought of Judaism as perpetuating ancient superstitions, and he was always much concerned with eradicating superstition from contemporary Christianity. He even found it hard to accept Roman Catholicism as properly Christian. These religious prejudices overlapped with a certain xenophobia. He was proud of being an Englishman of his day and age. He took no active interest in overseas missions and expressed gloomy sympathy for clergymen who had to serve in non-Christian countries. Despite his professed internationalism and his support for such causes as Indian nationalist aspirations, he had his share of the nineteenth-century's patronising attitude to 'lesser breeds without the law', even if they now happened to live in England. But, as one who had made his own way in life, he would also have recognised that many of his Jewish fellow citizens had been equally or more successful; and here perhaps another prejudice came into play. He was consistently hostile to 'big business' which he tended to regard as inhuman and oppressive, almost by definition. Certainly, whatever his reasons, he used to tease my mother for having 'a strange liking for Jews'. But my mother, having been born and brought up in Manchester, was much better acquainted than he was with the Anglo-Jewish community. C. P. Scott, the editor of the *Manchester Guardian*, who contributed so much to the Balfour Declaration, was a close family friend. My mother's first cousin had moreover married Arthur Schuster, Professor of Physics at Manchester University and a first-generation Jewish immigrant from Germany, and with him had been the first Manchester family to befriend the future President of Israel, Chaim Weizmann, when in 1903 he arrived as a Russian-speaking and doubtless bewildered demonstrator in the chemistry department there. The Schusters practised Anglicanism but were none the less dedicated Zionists

So I suppose that from this parental mixture I had grown up with a passive disinterest in Jews but no active prejudice against them. In those days the upper-middle class were apt to speak slightingly of Jews and Jewishness, using the words as synonyms for behaviour like Shylock as indeed the *Oxford Dictionary* still does; but they did not often consciously mean what they said. Certainly, at school and university, it never occurred to me that Jewish fellow pupils, such as there were of them, belonged to a different race apart. When Stormont Mancroft died, it was reported that he had suffered greatly from anti-semitism at Winchester; as his contemporary there I never noticed anything of the kind and am astonished at the allegation. At Cambridge too, I saw a good deal, for example, of David Jacobson, a fine man later killed in the war, but I thought of him as an Etonian, a classical scholar and an impressive personality, but it hardly occurred to me that he was Jewish.

The first year that I spent my summer holidays in Bavaria trying to learn some German was 1936, the year of the Berlin Olympic Games, when Jesse Owens exploded the Nazis' racial theories of Aryan dominance. One was shocked, however, by notices at the entry to remote country villages proclaiming 'Juden nicht erwünscht'. But despite these intimations of inhumanity and although most of us undergraduates then were strongly anti-fascist and for that matter anti-Chamberlain, our hostility to Hitler was aroused more by his aggressions in Europe than by his persecution of the Jews. The Holocaust has since quite rightly come to be seen as a watershed in Jewish, and indeed in European, history. But, at the time, to the extent that we were aware of the concentration camps and their atrocities, we thought of them as instruments against opponents of the régime, rather than against the Jews as such. Our minds simply could not encompass the scale of the enormities which were being perpetrated and it was not until the liberation of Belsen, Buchenwald, Auschwitz and the rest that our eyes were fully opened to the truth. With hindsight we should never have been so blind, but we were not alone in our myopia.

Even so, I am ashamed to remember that when I was in Washington from 1946–48 and the Embassy was the target of Jewish protests against British policy in Palestine, I shared in the general anti-semitic reaction. Admittedly, one was partly influenced by reports of so-called terrorism by the Stern Gang and the Irgun, but even so the heart should not so easily have ruled the head. I am sorry too that at the time of Israel's independence in the spring of 1948 I was too busy getting married to take an interest in what was going on in the Middle East, not that I could have influenced events in any way.

It was not until 1952, when we went to Lebanon, that I began to have any inkling of the Arab-Israel problem. Even so, it is ironic now to remember that, when Hugh Gaitskell stayed with us in Beirut and, having a Jewish wife, took a strongly pro-Israel line, I did my utmost to convince him that the Arabs had a case too. With his usual charm and generosity of spirit, he seemed to accept that there were two sides to the question. But he made me think too. While we were there, also, and when my parents were staying with us, we drove down, with special military permits, through the Lebanese-Israel frontier to picnic at Capernaum on the shore of the Sea of Galilee. That journey was an eye-opener, as we left the stone-choked hillsides of southern Lebanon and came out into the flat, irrigated green swards of Israel. Here was the parable of the sower brought up to date.

In the Suez crisis of 1956, although not liking the operation itself, I realised that Israel was one country in the region with which many of our interests coincided. I do not remember when or how my attitude crystallised into a more positive attitude to Israel; but when the opportunity of serving at Tel Aviv arose, I embraced it eagerly.

But in this rather mixed-up state my equipment for a diplomatic mission to Israel was woefully inadequate. I knew that some of my predecessors had virtually gone native; others had unashamedly hated the place. It was not going to be easy to maintain the necessary objectivity, especially as Israel was hemmed in by enemies and one would not be able to drive across a frontier to take a deep breath and correct any imbalance in one's vision. But the first thing to do was my homework, reading papers and meeting people.

We had not foreseen the generosity and warmth with which the Anglo-Jewish community in London was to welcome and encourage us. People like Siegmund Warburg, Israel Sieff, Isaac Wolfson, Charles Clore and several members of the Rothschild family all went out of their way to be helpful and to share their knowledge and enthusiasm with us. With all of them and with others whom we were to meet in Israel itself we made lasting friendships.

There were also some enlightening stories. Israel Sieff told us how, in 1917, he and Chaim Weizmann had gone to see Lloyd George who, as was his wont, had given them an appointment at breakfast time. There was the Prime Minister, no doubt signing state papers with one hand and eating scrambled egg with the other. He looked up impatiently at the two Zionists and asked, 'Don't you know there's a war on? Can't you wait till the end of it for your national home?' Weizmann drew himself up to his considerable height and replied, 'Prime Minister, we have waited two thousand years and we are not going to wait any longer.' Oh, all right,' said Lloyd George, 'have your Balfour Declaration.'

Incidentally, this is perhaps a place to nail the story that, in the First World War, Weizmann refused to give the British Government the formula for acetone unless they agreed to a Jewish national home. This is a gross slander. Weizmann was devoted to Britain, which had given him refuge; he was not a huckster and would not have stooped to bargain on a matter of national security. Indeed, as I later wrote in an article in *Encounter*, he was deeply mortified when, after he became Israel's First President in 1948, the British Government pettily deprived him of his British passport.

Israel Sieff also took us round the Marks & Spencer headquarters in Baker Street and on the top floor showed us a replica of the trestle table which Michael Marks first set up as a stall in Leeds market place, with the sign 'Don't ask the price; everything on this stall one penny'.

Looking at the variety of merchandise on display, I said to Lord Sieff: 'Surely if Michael Marks was making a profit on some of these penny items, he must have made a loss on some others?' 'Don't you worry,' he replied, 'my father-in-law never made a loss on anything.'

Charles Clore was kind to us, both in Israel and after I retired. When he died, I went to his memorial service at the West London Synagogue. Taking a taxi to go home, I told the driver where I had been. 'Charles Clore?' he said. 'My uncle went to school with him and Lew Grade and Bernie Delfont in Bethnal Green.' I then said that the last time I had been in a synagogue was for the funeral of Jack Cohen of Tesco. 'Jack Cohen?' he answered. 'My father helped him push his first barrow in Bermondsey.' I said that the happiest moment of Cohen's life had been when he opened a store on that first barrow-pitch. 'There you are,' said my driver, 'Jack Cohen was always a happy man and Charles Clore was always miserable.' It is usually a 50–50 bet that a London taxi-driver will be Jewish. Another time I was paying my fare and found I was about to hand over an Israeli coin. 'Gimme that,' the driver cried. 'I nearly went out to fight for them in the Six-Day War.' Before I knew it, I was more or less holding a Zionist meeting on the pavement in South Kensington. I still have a tie-clip, by the way, given me by Jack Cohen, with the inscription YCDBSOYA, which he interpreted as 'You can't do business sitting on your – armchair.'

The other vital preparation for going to Israel was to learn some Hebrew. In Israel, Hebrew is not just a means of communication, it is a symbol of national unity. All immigrants are first sent to a language school, or Ulpan, to learn the Hebrew language as a criterion of citizenship. If one is not Jewish, a few words of Hebrew are welcomed out of all proportion and compensate for a multitude of oratorical deficiencies. It helped in London to have a pretty Israeli girl for a teacher, even if it made concentration on the language harder. At least I was able to present my letters to President Shazar in Hebrew and to tell him that I had been born in the year of the Balfour Declaration and married in the year of the foundation of the State of Israel. I must admit, however, that for my own benefit, instead of learning Hebrew, I might have done better to spend the time reading the Bible, which is the best history of the country and the best guide to it. If in Burgundy every village is a name on a bottle, in Israel every crossroads seems to be a verse from the Bible. After all, although nineteenth-century reductionist theologians had spent most of their time proving to their own satisfaction that the Bible stories were mythical at best, Israeli archaeologists of the twentieth century have succeeded in showing that most of them were factually correct.

Hebrew sometimes had practical uses. It once enabled me to persuade the Minister of Police to liberate from gaol the son of a distinguished Englishman, who was languishing there on drugs charges. But it has snags too. Once, scanning the English-language *Jerusalem Post*, I read that a British subject called Applejohn had been sent to prison. Storming down to the Embassy to ask why I had not been warned, I was told that they knew nothing of Applejohn; the only Englishman who had been imprisoned lately was O'Flanagan, about whom I was fully informed. Momentarily nonplussed, I suddenly saw the answer. O'Flanagan had been transliterated into Hebrew and then back again to English. There are no Hebrew vowels, F=P, G=J and so on. The two names were the same.

On another occasion our daughter Sarah was coming for her holidays. Some 25,000 Israelis then also had British nationality, but were expected to use their Israeli passports to travel in and out of the country, to make it easier to collect travel tax. The immigration officials looked suspiciously at Sarah's British passport and at her. 'Are you Israeli?' 'No.' 'Are you Jewish?' 'No.' 'Then why do you have a Hebrew name like Sarah Bar-Nes?' To make matters worse, 'Bar-Nes' means child of a miracle and we did not particularly want it thought that a child of ours could only have been born thanks to miraculous intervention.

Our youngest son was even harder pressed. When we arrived in Israel, he was just starting to read and write. So at Tabeetha, the Scottish school in Jaffa, they began by teaching him to write English from the left of the page and Hebrew from the right. When he became cross-eyed, we stopped the Hebrew.

That school, incidentally, had a romantic history. A hundred years earlier, a Scots girl had been told that if she stayed in Scotland she would only live for months, but in a warmer climate she might survive a year or two. So she went to the Holy Land and, seeing the lack of education for Arab girls, started a small school for them. Forty years later, she was still there, in excellent health, and by our day the school had two hundred pupils, drawn from over twenty nationalities, and was the only school outside Scotland still fully maintained by the Church of Scotland.

Israel taught me many things, not least never to generalise about Jews. So often one has been the only person in a room who was not Jewish. One looked round and saw people of every size, shape and colour of the rainbow. Never again could one say: Jews look like this, Jews think that, Jews do the other.

We arrived there in 1969 within two years of the Six-Day War. The Israelis were on top of the world: they had routed their enemies, God was on their side, the future was in their hands. But this was not a military camp. Israel was not a Sparta, but an Athens. Immense weight was placed on academic values. I forget the exact figures; but, if in the USA at that time one student in two received higher education, the figure in Israel was about one in four, but in Britain more like only one in seven. It was true that Israel had not won any Nobel Prizes, but this was largely because circumstances had forced her to concentrate on applied rather than pure science. But the standard is high and universities abound: one in Jerusalem, two in Tel Aviv, one each in Haifa and Beersheva, with post-graduate scientific bodies at the Weizmann Institute at Rehovot and the Technion at Haifa, and an Open University covering the whole country. All this is in accordance with the Jewish intellectual tradition: of six thinkers who each revolutionised his own academic discipline in the last two centuries, Marx, Pasteur, Darwin, Einstein, Freud and Keynes, it is significant that three of them were Jewish.

When Israel had proclaimed her independence in 1948, the members of the United Nations which had recognised her had been unwilling also to recognise Jerusalem as the capital, since the United Nations had proclaimed the city a *corpus separatum*. So it was the fate of our various Embassies to be located in or around Tel Aviv, while the Government had by now established itself in Jerusalem, all except, for security reasons, the Ministry of Defence. So, if one wanted to visit the Foreign Ministry, or call on another Minister, one had to drive all the way to Jerusalem, then a journey which could take an hour and a half. As I cannot read in a car without becoming seasick, I had to spend the time composing despatches which I never sent and speeches which I never delivered.

Israel was a place of high thinking and plain living, the same description incidentally which my father had applied to the Athenaeum in London when he put me up for membership. It was also a do-it-yourself country. Compared with most diplomatic posts, servants were few and far between and their hours of work statutorily restricted. One had to engage the butler before one invited the guests. But at least you could be sure for six months of the year that, if you invited two or three hundred people to a cocktail party, they could spread themselves over the garden without any risk of a rainstorm crowding them into the house. The house itself was all on one level and pretty small, until we managed to build on an extra bedroom and bathroom for visiting Ministers. We also extended the garden to an extra level which we christened the Piazza Barnese.

The garden itself was full of exotic flowers and we were woken every morning by a woodpecker in the flame-of-the-forest tree outside our window and could then watch the hoopoes preening themselves with crests erect on the lawn or a roller swooping in a flash of green and blue across the hedges of oleander.

Israel at that time had some outstanding personalities. Most of them were people who in their youth had dreamed dreams and seen visions, and had lived to see their dreams come true and their visions fulfilled, a reward given to few generations of mankind. Many of them had already lived three lives in one lifetime: somewhere perhaps in Poland or beyond the Pale of Settlement in Russia, then escaping from pogroms to Western Europe or to the United States and finally to the national home which they had themselves striven to build. They were not prepared to put that achievement at risk by allowing themselves again to be driven out of the promised land, to lead yet another life elsewhere. Security was their watchword and they were not going to gamble on their future. 'Reculez pour mieux sauter' was not their motto.

In this spirit, David Ben Gurion, whom I only met once on his kibbutz, Sde Boker, in the Negev desert, was to the end an admirer of Winston Churchill and of his determination in 1940 not to yield an inch of ground. But it was the same Ben Gurion who, while a fighter to his finger tips, had ensured from Israel's earliest days, in the famous Altalena incident, that terrorism should not prevail and the civil power would remain in control of the military. His vision was of a sovereign, secular democracy.

During our time in Israel the Prime Minister was Golda Meir. Although Ben Gurion had called her the only man in his Cabinet, she remained intensely feminine. As Prime Minister she wielded great authority and made it felt, but she still liked to be treated as a woman.

So much so that when I went to Holland and paid my first call on the Prime Minister there, I remarked without thinking that the last time I had called on a Prime Minister, I had kissed the Prime Minister on both cheeks. Dr Biesheuvel, a large, masculine figure, was clearly apprehensive of the tendencies of this new British envoy.

But I was not alone. When Henry Kissinger was working his famous Middle East shuttle service, a photograph was published showing him and President Sadat warmly embracing. Kissinger arrived in Israel next day and at the airport advanced to greet Golda Meir in the same way. On all the microphones, she was heard to say 'But Henry, I thought you only kissed men.'

Life with Golda Meir was not all kisses. She had been a Zionist almost since Zionism was invented. She had heard all the questions and thought she knew all the answers. Like Winston Churchill and the British Empire, she had not become Prime Minister of Israel to preside over its dissolution. Not for her now to jeopardise the future of her country by taking even calculated risks, although in earlier days she had undertaken a hazardous journey to treat with King Abdullah of Jordan. Now her main concern was to keep a safe pair of hands and in Israel's precarious situation who could blame her?

A senior Israeli official once warned me that the politicians I was dealing with were mostly audodidacts. But this was certainly not true of Abba Eban, the Foreign Minister, who was the product of a brilliant Cambridge career, having become a Fellow of his college there. But he had identified himself with Israel from the end of his wartime military service in the Middle East and had held ambassadorial rank from the tender age of thirty-three. An eloquent orator, he was also a formidable diplomatic operator and an accomplished multilinguist. He kept one on one's toes but it was a pleasure to deal with a skilled raconteur with a delightful sense of humour and a surprise to find an Israeli Minister who knew the latest Test Match score before one did oneself.

More autodidactic was Moshe Dayan, Defence Minister during all my time. He was agreeably informal: indeed my first official call on him was paid in the bar of the King David Hotel. The boyish charm was an asset, although in some ways he seemed never quite to have grown up and enjoyed playing cops and robbers, with other little games, amatory and archaeological, on the side. In my day he was uncrowned king of the defence establishment and it was sad that his well-deserved military reputation later came unstuck in the Yom Kippur war and that he then deserted his party to take the Foreign Ministry under Begin.

One of the most remarkable men in Israel never served as a Minister. Indeed, Teddy Kollek, the quasi-eternal Mayor of Jerusalem, often found himself at loggerheads with the Government of his country. But he was a citizen of no mean city and in that city his achievements were legendary. They supplied a practical lesson on Jewish-Arab co-existence, a lesson which could well have been applied much further afield. When his own Government starved him of credits, he exploited his abilities as a world-class 'schnorrer', as fund-raisers were known in Yiddish, to enhance the beauty and emphasise the destiny of his thrice-Holy City. 'Si monumentum requiris . . . ' That epitaph might do him justice. But, as a pioneer in Arab-Jewish friendship, he would have been a strong candidate for the Nobel Peace Prize and, on a more practical level, I am not alone in regretting that he never became Prime Minister of Israel.

Probably, though, the most powerful man then in Israel was Pinhas Sapir, the Finance Minister. Almost unknown abroad, he ruled the Labour Party, the Government and the country out of his little black pocket book. I had some animated dealings with him over British investment in Israel and he could not or would not understand why other Governments did not give instructions to their industries in the same way as he did. As economic dictator and party boss, he presided over a system so personally centralised that it could not possibly survive him.

Thus it was in 1977 that, with the Yom Kippur debacle of 1973 in quite recent memory and suspicion of the Government's finger in every financial pie, the electorate turned against the Labour Party and brought Menachem Begin to power. This was long after my time; but I had known and had easy relations with Mr Begin when I was there. Despite his reputation as a ruthless resistance fighter, he was at heart a fastidious and old-fashioned Polish lawyer, with a love-hate complex towards Britain. He had fought against us but admired our way of life. In later years I was to call on him twice when he was Prime Minister; the first time he started by discussing the first chapter of Genesis and the second the text of Shakespeare's *Julius Caesar*, on both of which he knew far more than I did. His rise to power was the culmination of thirty patient years, almost all in opposition, during which he had cultivated the underdog Sephardic or oriental community, who had often been treated as second-class citizens, while the Ashkenazi establishment of European origin ruled the roost. As the Sephardic birthrate far outran the Ashkenazi, by 1977 the underdogs had become the majority and swept Begin into the Prime Minister's office. It was not just a vote against the Labour Party but a positive choice for change with Likud.

The Israeli electoral system of absolute proportional representation, with the whole country a single constituency, notoriously leads to a proliferation of small parties and thus to coalition Governments based on compromise and almost always including religious representatives who could demand a price for their cooperation in the shape of concessions to orthodoxy. Another effect which is less widely noted is that, with seats in the Knesset allocated in accordance with the proportion of votes won, membership of Parliament depends on an individual's place on his party's list. This is decided by the party bosses, so that a candidate has to charm those bosses rather than electors in a constituency and can be returned to Parliament without ever showing his face to the populace. Not a healthy arrangement.

With the system as it was, Anglo-Israeli trade took up much time. Major contracts could not often be secured without official help. This was not surprising, given the importance of trade to the Israeli economy. Golda Meir used to say that she had it in for Moses because he had carted the people of Israel round the desert for forty years and then put them down in the only part of the Middle East where there was no oil. Not only no oil; no steel, no grain and not much fresh water. So at any given time if Israel's exports amount to x, her imports are likely to cost 2x. As the balance of trade has to be made up by aid, the incentive is to keep down the imports; and competition among countries exporting to Israel is keen. Israel is not the only country lacking raw materials; Japan is another, which has conspicuously succeeded. But, unlike Israel, Japan does not have to spend 40% of her national income on defence.

Israel was a fascinating place in which to live and to travel, a beautiful country ranging from market-garden in the north to desert in the south, with history in every footstep and plenty of modern excitements. We were there between the 1967 and 1973 wars, but violence was never far from our minds, with the war of attrition with Egypt, with aircraft hijacked to Dawson's Field, with Japanese gunmen spraying machine-gun fire across the arrival concourse at Tel Aviv airport, or with King Hussein suppressing the PLO in which came to be called Black September, 1970. On the last occasion, there were vantage-points in Israel from which one could see the tank battle in Jordan, so that we were in a better position to report to the Foreign Office than our Embassy in Amman, who had mostly to take cover underground.

There was much pleasure too. At least one of our guests swam on four successive days in the Mediterranean Sea, the Dead Sea, the Red Sea and the Sea of Galilee. Both the Dead Sea and the Sea of Galilee are well below what is normally called sea-level. Once, driving our five-year-old son down to the Sea of Galilee, we passed the sign saying that we were then going below sea-level and he asked us urgently to shut the car windows. On arrival at the seashore we told him that this was where Jesus had walked on the water; he planted his foot firmly on the surface and, when it sank through, asked: 'Mummy, was Jesus joking?'

By the Dead Sea a visit to the Massada mountain-fortress was obligatory. Usually we had to climb up the cliff. There was a cable car but we thought it soft to use it. But once, when our Air Commander-in-Chief from Cyprus was visiting, the Israeli Air Force flew us in a helicopter to land on the top. Over the Judaean desert we passed a flock of vultures to the alarm of my aviator companions: one vulture hitting one helicopter blade and we should drop like a stone. But we landed safely. My diplomatic function was to provide the picnic and I handed round Israeli vin rosé, affectionately known to us as Rosie of Carmel, to all including the pilot. Inspired by this, after luncheon, instead of lifting the helicopter gently upwards, he drove it straight at the edge of the cliff and then flew at zero altitude above the distinctly choppy waves of the Dead Sea. Helicopters should not be fuelled on pink wine. But, undeterred by this, the Air Marshal's ADC married our eldest daughter a year or so later.

I was not supposed to show my face officially in the administered territories: Sinai, the West Bank and Gaza. But they well repaid incognito visits. Early on we drove into the desert to see the Russian-made tanks, still lying in the sand where the Egyptians had lost them in the Six Day War. Rounding one large sand-dune we found three Arabs sitting in leather armchairs and smoking cigars, for all the world like clubmen in St James's Street. To this day I do not know how they got there; I do not think they were a mirage.

Further afield, we once flew in a small aircraft to the monastery of Santa Caterina, under Mount Sinai, and then on to Sharm-el-Sheikh. At the monastery our guide, a Greek-Orthodox monk, announced that he was Cypriot born and wanted to renew his British passport. Preserving my incognito, I asked two colleagues to go with him to find the passport; when they came back and I asked why they had been so long, they explained that they had been to his cell and had difficulty finding the passport under all the copies of *Playboy* magazine.

Jericho, with the remains of a city 8,000 or more years old, was another must. Once, driving up the dusty road back to Jerusalem, my car for some reason would only go at five miles an hour until we came to Bethany, where Lazarus was raised from the dead, when the engine suddenly spurted into life and the car leaped forward. From that day on that car was rechristened Lazarus. Another time, to avoid the dust, we took the back road and, rounding one corner, came on some four hundred storks feeding in the grass. We drove up close and still they went on eating. But when my wife said she must photograph them and stepped out of the car, every stork within range took off. I can only assume that their hereditary internal computers are programmed against human beings, but the programming was done before the invention of the motor car.

There were some hilarious occasions with visitors from England. I remember Isaiah Berlin coming to lecture at the Weizmann Institute one Christmas Eve on Disraeli, Marx and Hess – Hess the Zionist, not the Nazi. Knowing something of the first two but nothing of Hess, we broke our Christmas holiday to hear him. Isaiah spoke for an hour non-stop on Disraeli, took a breath, went on for another half-hour on Marx, then said he had no time to talk about Hess and sat down.

On another occasion Arnold Goodman came out for the opening of the Jerusalem Theatre. We joined him as he was being interviewed by a young girl from the *Jerusalem Post*. 'Is this your first visit to Israel, Lord Goodman?' 'No, I have been here several times.' 'How is that, Lord Goodman?' 'Well, after all as a Jew . . . ' 'Lord Goodman, you are a Jew and you are a Lord?'

In less exalted company, we took our eldest daughter to join an archaeological dig outside Beersheba. After we had passed a bucketful of bones, reported to be those of last year's excavators, we met a young Englishman pushing a huge barrow of rubble. Trying to show an intelligent interest, I asked the date of his pit. 'Fourth century.' Still trying to be bright, I asked 'B.C. or A.D.?' 'I don't know; we haven't had that lecture yet.'

An incidental amusement in Tel Aviv was the night-club kept by Mandy Rice-Davies, to which we sometimes took visitors from Britain. I thought she was rather a nice, warm-hearted young woman. But then I would, wouldn't I?

One uncovenanted bonus accrued when we gave a garden party for Cancer Relief and engaged a young Israeli entertainer. His name was Uri Geller. There he was, reading thoughts, bending spoons and stopping watches in our back garden, with our eldest daughter Patricia acting as plumber's mate. We like to think we helped to launch him on his glittering career.

All this no doubt sounds very frivolous. But we did quite a lot of work as well. Indeed, twice in three years we had to forgo our summer holiday on account of a political crisis. One was frequently being called to account for some allegedly adverse vote in the United Nations or, less justifiably, for some report on the BBC, which no one outside England will ever believe is not an official organ of the British Government. Indeed, I was inclined to think that too often on these occasions, by over-reacting, the Israelis advertised their failures at the bar of world opinion and would have been wiser to cloak them with oblivion. We were constantly under pressure, too, to supply military equipment, notably Chieftain tanks. But, although much of one's energy was absorbed in trade promotion, this was one export we were disinclined to push, lest it led to an Arab oil boycott which in turn could entail a sterling devaluation as in 1967.

But, despite these recurrent frictions, we met with immense goodwill. Israel has not forgotten the troubles of the Mandate or the indifference of British Governments to the problems of Jewish immigration during and after the Holocaust. But she remembers the Balfour Declaration too and knows that she shares with Britain a tradition of democracy and the rule of law. Indeed, much Israeli legal procedure is based on the legacy of British practice during the inter-war years. With a large community of immigrants from Britain, many of them with dual nationality, one had a ready-made English-speaking audience, even if not always uncritical of current British policy.

My immediate predecessor had been heard to say that, if Israel was a country of speechmakers and tree-planters, he would settle for tree-planting. I am sure he did not get away with it, and nor did I. All sorts of groups with British connections, and many without, chambers of commerce, rotary clubs, universities, schools and even forests dependent on British benefactors, all liked the British Ambassador to turn up and usually to 'say a few words'. But one could always be sure of a warm reception and usually a lively question time. There was rarely a dull moment. Once I even had to share a platform with Hubert Humphrey, who was doing the tour of the three 'I's, Ireland, Italy and Israel, then obligatory for American presidential candidates of the Democratic Party.

One was conscious all the time that to the Israelis their relations with the Americans loomed far larger than with us. Not only did they depend on the United States for massive financial aid, both official and private. Even more important, it was the United States who ultimately underpinned their security, despite their own self-confidence and self-reliance. My American colleague, Wally Barbour, had been there for many years and, being a genial character of enormous build, rather like Father Christmas without a beard, enjoyed immense prestige and was treated almost as an honorary godfather by Israeli officialdom. From time to time he would address them more like a heavy uncle, but this did not shake his well-deserved popularity.

The other super-power was not, of course, on stage but was always a shadow in the wings. Russia had nearly beaten America to the post in recognising Israel in 1948. Perhaps she saw Israel as a potential secular socialist client in a region then otherwise consisting almost entirely of feudal monarchies. Perhaps too she counted on a leadership composed more or less exclusively of one-time Russian subjects. Very few of the leaders were native-born, still fewer Sephardic of oriental origin. Indeed, it was said that if in America WASP meant white Anglo-Saxon Protestant, in Israel it signified white, Ashkenazi, Second-Aliyah with 'protection' - the second aliyah being the immigrants who came mostly from Russia and Poland in the wave from 1904 to 1914 and protection being a polite word for influence in high places. But the Russo-Israeli love affair, if ever there was one, did not last. From the start the Israelis had known that Washington counted to them for far more than Moscow and that America would be the main immediate source of immigrants as well as funds. As revolutions spread and displaced monarchies throughout the Arab world, the Russians increasingly transferred their attentions to those new régimes and eventually, with the outbreak of the Six-Day War in 1967, broke off diplomatic relations with Israel altogether.

But Israel can never ignore the deep reservoir of potential immigrants in the Jewish community of the former Soviet Union. For years virtually no exit visas were given. But while we were there, the tap was turned on again with a flow for a short time amounting to some 40,000 a year. Not all of them ended up in Israel and even those who did were not an entirely unmixed blessing. There was always the risk that some Soviet agents might be infiltrated among bona fide immigrants. But more difficult were the problems of assimilation. Israel likes her citizens to be Israelis *tout court* and to forget that they were ever Russians, Americans, Yemenites or whatever. Not for nothing has it been said that, if the United States is a melting-pot, Israel is a pressure-cooker. The normal procedure is for new immigrants first to be made proficient in Hebrew and then allocated in an even spread to settlements across the country. This did not at all suit the Russians who, even in their own country, tend to congregate in homogeneous groups. Of Russians abroad, it has been said that they do not so much go into exile as gather little Russias around them. They found it more comfortable to talk Russian cosily with old folks from home. Nor were they always politically adaptable: some were determined to leave 'socialism' behind them for good and found Israel still much too collectivist for their taste, while others, used to Big Brother telling them what to do, could not adjust to making their way in a free enterprise society. The classic example was of the barber, who was allotted a shop, a chair and all the tools of his trade; but when a month later the authorities came to ask how he was faring, he bemoaned the fact that they had given him all this but had not sent him any customers.

But the flow of *refusenik* refugees soon dried up, not to flow again until Gorbachev opened the sluice-gates under *perestroika* in 1989. Even then, it is hard to know how many Russian Jews were really animated by Zionism. Their main motive seems to have been to escape from the Soviet Union before the shutters closed again, either under Gorbachev or a less liberal successor. This desire was sharpened by a fear of rising anti-semitism. In hard times the Russians have always found the Jews convenient scapegoats. The Pamyat movement showed that this prejudice was still a useful political tool. What is more, now that *glasnost* allowed criticism of the system itself and the

1917 revolution from which it sprang, it began to be remembered how many Jews had shared in giving birth to the revolution, including seven members of the original Politburo. All this fanned the antisemitic flame and strengthened the determination of the Jews to go while the going was good.

But this did not mean that they necessarily wanted to go to Israel. They were voting with their feet against the Soviet Union, not for Israel. For some time they went first to Vienna or Bucharest, hoping there to turn right for the United States. It was only when the United States began to limit their number as immigrants that they settled for going straight to Israel. Even so, it is doubtful how far they will be ready to accept Israel as their final destination. They knew in Russia that they were Jews. But many of them had never attended a synagogue, few of them spoke Hebrew, probably only a handful had ever eaten a kosher meal. As one of them was reported as saying, 'In Russia I was a Jew; here in Israel I am a Russian.' They were going to be even less easy to assimilate than their predecessors nearly twenty years before, as they would always be looking over their shoulder at the chance of moving on further to the Western hemisphere. Nor were most of them, lawyers, doctors, professional people, the sort of material which could be easily adapted to Israel's defence requirements as volunteer soldiers or conscripts.

But much of that was after our time. We left Israel after three and a half engrossing years, personally and professionally. We had made many friends and enjoyed many new experiences. It had been the most stimulating assignment of our lives. From the point of view of the job, it had been necessary to make up one's own mind and express views from one's own corner. The Foreign Office is often accused of pro-Arab bias and Britain must always have regard to her interests in the Arab world, as elsewhere. But, like any other institution, the Foreign Office consists of individuals and, as there are a score of Arab countries but only one Israel, it is inevitable that at any given time there will be more decision-makers in London who have served in Arab capitals than in Tel Aviv. Some of them may indeed be biased but I suspect that it is much more a question of conditioned reflexes. In any case, those of us who were serving in the Middle East at the time had to report faithfully the attitudes of the countries to which we were accredited. One could not therefore from Israel expect to balance, in quantity at any rate, the reports and advice which flowed daily into London from one's own colleagues in surrounding posts. But at least it followed that one could not just send telegrams on the theme of 'me too'; one had to try to keep thinking independently. Even so, there remained the risk of one's own reflexes becoming conditioned and that is why it seemed sensible to leave before that happened.

Israel could also, it must be said, become a bit claustrophobic. One could not, as we had in Germany or were to do again in Holland, step into the car and just drive across the nearest frontier. The frontiers were, at least nominally, war-zones. Or, even if one could have arranged a diplomatic *laissez-passer*, one would at once have been suspect for carrying messages or some other clandestine activity. So Cyprus became our regular safety-valve, before the Ledra Palace Hotel in Nicosia was riddled with bullets. Towards the end of our three and a half years, we grew rather more relaxed and flew both to Istanbul and to Iran, in flights carefully avoiding Arab air-space. We are glad to have visited Istanbul, with its churches, mosques and museums, but even more to have seen Isfahan, Shiraz and Persepolis before the advent of the Ayatollah made such tourism inadvisable. At the very end we crossed into Jordan to visit Petra, nearly disgracing ourselves by toasting each other in Hebrew at the Philadelphia Hotel in Amman. Looking back, I wish we had been more adventurous.

During those three and a half years, man went to the moon, the President of the United States went to Communist China and Britain was admitted to the European Community. If such things could happen in that short time, it is hard to believe that it will ultimately be beyond the wit of man to solve the problems of the Middle East. But, alas, despite the years which have followed, they do not seem much nearer to a solution. Thanks to the generosity of the Rothschild family, I have been lucky enough to serve on the Council of the Open University of Israel and by regular visits to keep in touch with people and events there. Though much is taken, much abides. Israel is no longer a pioneer society; it has become much more of a consumer society. Fewer people now ask what they can do for their country day by day; more are inclined to ask what their country can do for them. There are probably more Israelis going abroad more or less permanently than, Russians apart, there are new immigrants coming into the country. One cannot altogether blame them for that, given the economic pressures of inflation, the continued absence of a peaceful settlement and the constant dangers of the surrounding insecurity. To some extent Israel has been her own enemy: the campaign of 1982 in Lebanon, for example, lost her her David image and made her look distressingly like Goliath. Such events have been controversial within the country itself too; when we lived there, you could scratch any Israeli and receive an identical answer, in essence the school solution. Nowadays one is just as likely to witness a fierce argument between hawks and doves. Opinion in the country has polarised and the so-called Government of National Unity between Likud and Labour was a misnomer from the start. National Disunity would have been a better description.

Not only has public opinion polarised. It has shown the effects of the *intifada* and of the violent Israeli reaction to it. This was partly to be expected. Israel's military manpower is limited. Her defence forces are trained to protect the country's territorial integrity at the frontiers, which, in effect, means to shoot at sight. That is no way to control riotous crowds. But Israel cannot afford a separate police force for internal security. She has to use her army. This, together with the fact that most Israeli soldiers are young, inexperienced conscripts, goes some way to explaining the imbalance between Israeli and Palestinian casualties. Admittedly, many *intifada* deaths are of Palestinians killed by other Palestinians. But an outsider cannot help feeling that it ought to be possible to resist stone-throwing youths without killing so many of them; or at least, if there is to be so strong a reaction, it should be accompanied by a more visible effort to negotiate and seek a peaceful solution.

Quite apart from the *intifada*, the hostility of most of the Arab world remains unabated. It is mitigated to some extent by inter-Arab dissensions and there is little sign of a concerted Arab strategy against Israel, for whose military prowess her neighbours have a healthy respect. Nor would a combined assault have much prospect of success without the participation of Egypt, which still retains the tenuous relations with Israel established at Camp David.

But all this may be wishful thinking. Logic does not always prevail, least of all in the Middle East. There are other unfavourable portents too. Despite the influx of Soviet immigrants, who are not in any case an unmixed blessing, the long-term demographic trends are not in Israel's favour. It is true that the Soviet Union, with more pressing domestic preoccupations, has withdrawn material support from its

Middle Eastern clients; but this in itself reduces Soviet power to influence them towards moderate policies. The other super-power, too, is showing impatience at Israel's reluctance to engage in the peace process which the US Government itself has sponsored. Nor is it only the US Government whose support is being eroded; the American Jewish community is also increasingly voicing its reservations about Israeli policies and it is all too likely that, as the older generation gives way to the new, memories will fade and support be further eroded.

The Gulf crisis has changed matters somewhat. Israel has earned merit for her restraint in the face of Iraqi scud attacks. The PLO is discredited by its support for Saddam Hussein. Jordan's voice is weaker too. Divisions in the Arab world have been sharpened. An even-handed approach should be easier to undertake. Obviously, for those of us in the outside world, with knowledge not only of the Holocaust but of the shameful treatment meted out to Jews over the centuries, it would be unthinkable to abandon Israel or to let her go under. Nor can we bludgeon Israel into making peace; the carrot is mightier than the stick. Experience has taught me that it is counter-productive to tell Israelis what to do.

Nevertheless, something is required of Israel herself too. For all her continuing dependence on outside support, she is no longer entirely on the receiving end of history. She cannot continue indefinitely, in a world of fading memories, to cash cheques on the Holocaust. She has built a strong nation and is now as much the subject as the object of the sentence. She has shown this in all her wars and undoubtedly, despite the polarisation of her domestic policies, the nation would again, in any emergency, unite in patriotic defence of the national cause against external threat. But with modern military technology a threat can develop very rapidly and the Yom Kippur War showed how near a surprise attack can come to success, before outside intervention can be brought to bear.

The Gulf war in turn has shown that, in the missile age, security is no longer spelt 't–e–r–r–i–t–o–r–y'. Israel would be little safer with her frontier on the Euphrates than with it on the Jordan. What matters is not lines on maps but the attitude of peoples on either side of these lines. In these circumstances, the exchange of land for peace is a much more attractive proposition.

It is therefore all the more important that the Israelis should recognise the need for compromise and accept that jaw-jaw is better than war-war. Peace is not an event but a process. The process needed to be started and it is incumbent on all men of goodwill to do what they can to carry it forward.

9
Going Dutch

At first sight no two countries could be more unlike than Israel and Holland. But look a bit closer. Both are small countries at the edge of large continents, both depend substantially on overseas trade, both have had little more than a generation of industrial production, both are intensely concerned with religion, both have large tracts of their territory below sea-level, both conduct a ceaseless struggle with nature, the Israelis against the desert and the Dutch against the sea. It is said that Holland is the only country which has added ten per cent. to its territory by means other than conquest. It is perhaps a coincidence that, of all European countries, Holland has been the most consistently friendly to Israel.

Nonetheless, when we moved from Israel, which was fairly eventful, to Holland we thought that by comparison it would be a quiet place where the dust settled. How wrong can you be? Within quick succession came a British aircraft hijacked to Amsterdam, the chapel congregation seized as hostages by inmates of the Hague prison, the French Ambassador holed up in his office for four days by Japanese gunmen, a siege of the Indonesian Consulate-General by Moluccans, then the capture of a train and its passengers by the same Moluccans and finally the brutal murder of my successor, Richard Sykes, at his own front door.

So the poet Heine was hardly right when he said that, if the end of the world was approaching, he would go to Holland, as everything always happened there fifty years later than anywhere else. It was in any case a quite unfair comment, at least as far as Dutch relations with England are concerned. One has only to look at Dutch styles of painting or building to see how the Dutch landscapists of the seventeenth century are reflected in the English of the eighteenth, or how Dutch architecture of the seventeenth century is known in England as 'Queen Anne'. Indeed, as George Trevelyan says in his *English Social History*, 'throughout the seventeenth century it was .. to Holland that

Englishmen looked for new ideas in religion, politics, agriculture, land-draining, gardening, commerce, navigation, philosophy, science and art'. A comprehensive and formidable catalogue.

The civilisation of Holland owes much to the fact that she has always been ready to open her doors to refugees from all directions. This was due partly to genuine humanitarianism, partly to enlightened self-interest. The arrival of the Huguenots after the revocation of the Edict of Nantes represented a great accretion of moral and commercial strength. Many of them, notably weavers and gardeners, bankers and silversmiths, were later to find their way to London in the wake of William III of Orange. But earlier, in the days of the first Stuarts, refugees had moved in the opposite direction, as Puritans fled from persecution to a more congenial religious climate in Holland. One group of them, in fact, had planned to emigrate directly from Amsterdam to America and it was only when their Dutch ship failed to start that they had to return to Plymouth and catch the *Mayflower*.

Another feature which Holland and Israel have in common is an electoral system of total proportional representation. In each case the whole country is a single constituency and membership of Parliament is determined by party lists. It follows in each case that there is a proliferation of small parties and as a result every Government has to be a coalition. In Holland each coalition tends to take six months or more of horse-trading after an election to put it together. Thus, at elections the voters are not able to make a choice of Prime Minister or even of governing party. The Prime Minister and his Government only emerge after the electoral sums have been laboriously calculated and conclusions drawn in long drawn-out negotiations.

Our time in Holland covered the period between two elections and coincided almost exactly with the term of Joop den Uyl's Government, socialistic but including Christian Democrats. In opposition were the Liberals, who in British terms would be more like right-wing Conservatives. Our arrival at the end of 1972 also coincided with Britain's entry into the European Community. This was a moment of high hopes. We hoped that our economic problems would be solved at a stroke, as we came in to share the exponential growth of the Community up to that time. The Dutch, for their part, hoped that we should help to democratise the Community, both by strengthening its parliamentary institutions and by championing the rights of the smaller members against the fear of a Franco-German hegemony.

Then came the Yom Kippur War and those hopes were all disappointed. Our material interests led us to share the French attitude towards the belligerents more than that of the Dutch. Indeed for a time Holland found itself isolated as the victim of an Arab boycott. The rise in the price of oil which followed the war put paid to any hopes that economic growth would continue at the same rate as during the previous decade. Soon afterwards the Labour Government came to power in London, committed to renegotiation of the terms of our membership of the Community and the referendum which followed it. From the point of view of our fellow members the referendum gave the right result but this was not a happy time for any British representative in a Community capital.

A problem of a different kind had arisen when we joined the Community and decided to stage a celebration in London called 'Fanfare for Europe'. A feature of this was to be an exhibition of one artistic masterpiece from each member country of the newly enlarged Community. Britain, needless to say, showed a Stubbs picture of a horse. The French sent Georges de la Tour's *Tricheur*; whether this was an indirect allusion to *perfide Albion* was not clear. Italy provided the Michelangelo bust of Brutus from Florence, the Danes a prehistoric hunting-horn and so on. From the Dutch we had asked for Rembrandt's picture of his son Titus as a Franciscan in a brown cowl. 'Of course,' said the Dutch, whose last major loan of a Vermeer to the Brussels Europalia had been cut from its frame, 'provided you insure it for £2 million there and back from hook to hook.' 'Oh no', we replied, 'the British Government never insures, but we shall provide you with an indemnity against loss.' 'But,' said they, 'what if your Parliament refuses to confirm and vote the indemnity?' 'Don't worry,' we answered, confident that at that time the Government had a safe majority 'Parliament will do what is asked of it'. Luckily this argument was accepted. The picture duly came and eventually was returned safely to its hook in the Rijksmuseum.

Politically, with our entry into the Community, The Hague became largely a diplomatic observation post. We had few bilateral problems with the Dutch Goverment, who were consistently friendly and helpful. More and more of the business of international negotiating was Community machinery at Brussels. This is an aspect of a general trend whereby diplomacy has become more multilateral than bilateral and we live largely in an age of diplomacy by standing conference. This did not mean that we always saw eye to eye with the Dutch on Community matters, least of all on the Common Agricultural Policy. Many a time would Dutch officials say to me 'Don't you have a farming lobby too?' and I would answer 'Yes, but we have a much stronger consumer lobby.'

Bilateral economic relations were also important. At that time, Holland, though a country of only some fourteen million inhabitants, ranked regularly third or fourth in our world export league table. Part of this trade consisted of internal transfers within the Anglo-Dutch multinational giants, Royal Dutch/Shell and Unilever. Part of it too was transit trade through Rotterdam, still the largest port of the world . The Netherlands form the gateway to Europe and particularly to the Eldorado of the German hinterland.

This massive flow of trade followed well-worn channels and, unlike in Israel, there was little need for ambassadorial intervention, except sometimes to secure defence contracts. I like to think that the purchase of Tyne–Olympus turbines for the Dutch frigates was secured when we had half the board of Rolls-Royce and half the top brass of the Dutch Navy sitting round our luncheon table.

Nonetheless, it was useful and agreeable to keep in touch with the commercial and industrial life of the country. Dutch bankers are shrewd and well-informed sources of information. Dutch industry is innovative and its labour relations were excellent. This was largely due to the flourishing system of the Works Council, or Ondernemingsraad, by which industrial democracy is effected at works level and workers' loyalty is directed to the company rather than to the national trade unions, thus, it is to be hoped, minimising the risk of widespread strikes or secondary boycotts. To assist in this endeavour, the Dutch, like the Germans, have their own version of Mitbestimmung, with two-tier boards and workers' representatives on the supervisory boards. Another feature of Dutch labour relations was the work structuring adopted by firms like Philips, with people producing not as individuals but in groups, so that one person could either produce a single television set by himself or could devote himself to producing the same component for all the sets made by the group. Philips claimed that this flexibility led to much less sickness or absenteeism than the assembly line system immortalised by Charlie Chaplin in *City Lights*.

One had to remember that for centuries the Dutch had been a

trading people relying on their overseas empire. When that empire came to an end as a result of the Second World War, they saw that they must take to manufacture. But the country rested both physically and financially on a bubble of national gas, which swelled their exports and also reduced their energy import bill. This inevitably strengthened the guilder and meant that, when the gas ran out, Dutch exports might find themselves priced out of the markets. There have been some signs of this already.

But all this meant that we had some enjoyable times visiting factories. One of the first was the AKZO subsidiary, Organon, at Oss. We had hardly arrived before we were all given a pregnancy test, which, I am glad to say, both my wife and I passed with flying colours. Then we were shown a frozen rat, which was being studied to show which organ an isotope ingested with its food had reached; we still have a rather elegant and transparent plastic plate with an infinitesimally thin slice of that rat embedded in it. Finally, at the same factory, we actually witnessed a monkey playing the organ. He had electrodes fitted into his brain, so that when he pressed a particular stop and was rewarded for it by some succulent morsel, one could tell which part of his brain was brought into service and this knowledge could be used for human medical research. He showed every sign of enjoying himself and our applause.

In the same factory we were taken into a room where they were packing 'the pill'. Hundreds and thousands of contraceptive pills were pouring through hoppers. I suddenly noticed a small cage in the corner of the ceiling, containing two white mice and asked what they were doing there. We were told: 'They are male mice and when they start to show secondary female sexual characteristics, we change the shift of packers.' I left that room rather hastily.

Our commercial activities were subsumed in the vigorous Netherland-British Chamber of Commerce, of which Prince Bernhard was the honorary President. The Prince has done great things as an Ambassador for Dutch enterprise and it was a sad experience to live in Holland during the saga of his connections with Lockheed. But nothing became him in his business life like the ending of it. He confessed, he apologised and he resigned his business appointments. No one could ask more than that and, as one who has received much kindness from him, I believe that the Dutch people have now forgiven and forgotten and taken him to their hearts again. Holland is not a monarchy so much as a republic with a royal family. The royal family say as much themselves and are none the less popular for that.

Another and pleasant dimension of life at The Hague was our contact with the British military authorities in Germany, where the Dutch also had a contingent serving. We had regular meetings with the Commanders-in-Chief of Rhine Army and Second Tactical Air Force, either at their headquarters at Mönchen-Gladbach or in one of the capitals concerned, Bonn, Brussels or The Hague itself. These connections also kept us in fairly constant touch with Dutch defence people too, not only in trying to sell them hardware.

The Dutch were loyal members of NATO and indeed, in Dirk Stikker and Josef Luns, produced two of its more effective Secretaries-General. In a way, this was surprising because they are far from being a militaristic nation and for a century or more after the Napoleonic Wars had pursued a policy of neutrality, maintaining that policy throughout the First World War. It was only the German assault on 10 May 1940, which had pitchforked the country, willy-nilly, into belligerency and resistance to occupation. The momentum thus generated carried the Dutch forward into the Western European Union and the North Atlantic Alliance, against the weight of the national tradition. The loss of their overseas empire meant that they saw their role as confined to European defence and there were elements of the population for whom 'nuclear' was a dirty word, both in its military and civil aspects. But this did not deter successive Dutch Governments from playing their full part in the Western alliance and faithfully supporting its strategy.

One fascinating experience was when their Chief of Defence Staff, General Robbie Wijting, invited us to spend an evening with members of the *réseaux* who had organised the underground escape of himself and Allied fugitives through occupied territory during the war and on to England where the Dutch Government was in exile. It was both heartening and depressing to find these people, who must have run hair-raising risks for years, settled down without any apparent reward into quite humdrum occupations in post-war civilian life, such as selling carpets.

As base for all these activities, and many more, we had a splendid house in The Hague at 12 Westeinde. It had been rebuilt in the eighteenth century by a Spanish Ambassador, but there had been a house on the same site since the Middle Ages. It had belonged to the

Assendelft family. In the sixteenth century the young Assendelft heir had spent the night at a French country inn, where the landlord had a pretty daughter. Some months later the innkeeper asked him what his intentions were towards the pregnant girl. He dutifully married her. But, once installed as Countess Assendelft, she did not take to high society and found time hanging heavy on her hands. So to keep herself occupied, she took to counterfeiting the coinage. In those days of the Spanish occupation, this was a capital offence and she was duly sentenced to be burnt at the stake. But despite her misdemeanours, she was still a devout Catholic and feared that, if she was consumed by fire, she would be unable to take her place in one piece at the resurrection on the Day of Judgement. She appealed to the Queen of Hungary, then regent of the Netherlands, who commuted the sentence to death by the water treatment. This revolting fate consisted of having water poured down your throat until you could survive it no longer. It sounds no great improvement on burning at the stake.

The consequence was that her ghost was still believed to haunt the house. One difficulty was that when the house had been rebuilt the level of the floors had been raised. She still walked on the old floors, so that only the top half of her protruded above the present boards. Having regard to the nature of her death, she therefore made her presence felt by watery manifestations. There was certainly one occasion when we had the table laid for a large luncheon party and a torrent of water suddenly descended on it through the ceiling above. But we satisfied ourselves that it was due to faulty plumbing.

The ghost was well-known and at least one of my predecessors had had a ceremony of exorcism performed. Indeed, it became rather tedious to be asked about the ghost and I was forced to take the line that I was more interested in the spirits in the wine cellar than those in the house above. It was also a bit of a bore that people never seemed to express appreciation of our charming company but only for our lovely house, making us feel like Disraeli's description of the occupants of the Treasury Bench as 'transient and embarrassed phantoms'.

But it certainly was a fine house and it contained some lovely things, both pictures and furniture. There came a time when many of them needed expert attention and three representatives of an English firm of restorers came to spend several weeks in the house making repairs and touching up decoration. They strung up a series of lights in the enormous attic of the house, and worked from dawn to dusk at their various tasks, to the admiration, for their diligence, of the resident people of the Embassy. One portrait was of an English seventeenth-century beauty, attributed to the School of Lely. I came down one morning to find that the restorer working on the frame with his gold paint had deleted the 'school'. The picture overnight became a genuine Lely and, as far as I know, remains so to this day.

It was also a very big house. My wife assured me that twenty-three people could sleep in it at once and that they did so for our eldest daughter's wedding. There were said to be sixty-three rooms, including the cellars, and certainly several that I never saw during the five years we were there. For that wedding, we followed a local custom and hired a white coach with two white horses and a female coachperson in uniform, in which we trundled through the streets, followed by a black coach with black horses containing the bridesmaids. This journey had to be done twice, first to the civil wedding by the burgomaster and then, after an interval suspended between being the single and the married state, to the English church. The burgomaster of The Hague, in a delightful speech in English, greeted our daughter, recently arrived from Israel, with 'shalom' and her airman bridegroom with 'happy landings'. Robin Woods took the church service and a Royal Air Force contingent blew trumpets and held swords over the bridal pair.

But living at Westeinde 12 was rather like living in a hotel. One was never quite sure who was staying in the house, which lent itself splendidly to entertaining, especially as it boasted the only ballroom in town, the scene of many a riotous assembly. Many guests left happy memories behind them. Chief of them all was Queen Elizabeth the Queen Mother, who had been going to fly out for the day to reopen the Scots church at Amsterdam, lunching with us and allowing us to give a drinks party first for the British official family. But when the Queen of Holland asked the Queen Mother to luncheon, I had to admit that Queen trumped Ambassador and we should sadly have to abandon our own party. Not a bit of it. The Queen Mother at once undertook to extend her visit, spend the night in our house and have the drinks party before dinner instead. Not only did Her Majesty speak to every one of the 200 guests, she insisted on speaking tête-à-tête individually to the butler, chauffeur, chef and social secretary, giving each a personal present commensurate with their years of service to the Embassy, and before dinner she invested a Dutchman with the CBE. No wonder she is so greatly loved.

Other random memories are of Yehudi Menuhin staying for a week, sallying forth to give a concert in a different Dutch town every night, returning after midnight and giving a violin lesson in the ballroom each morning to a former pupil from his Stoke d'Abernon school, for whom he had into the bargain taken a room with his bride, also a former pupil, at the Hôtel des Indes and tickets for each of his concerts as a wedding present. The true milk of human kindness. Arthur Rubinstein called Menuhin a bad Jew, with which I for one should not agree, but he is certainly a fine human being. Or on another occasion, of Christopher Soames offering to remove one of our baths, as the only one in Europe big enough to fit him. Or of Tony Benn asking for milk and an electric kettle, to match his own tea-bags, rather than whisky and soda, in his bedroom. Or of one Minister's private secretary, who asked the butler to put two bottles of our best Burgundy in their luggage, 'without telling the Ambassador'. Or of Terry Lewin, then Vice-Chief of Naval Staff, allowing our younger son, aged nine, to beat him at chess. Or of the visiting preacher who kept us awake as he paced up and down one of the spare rooms for half the night, rehearsing his sermon. Or two days before we left Holland, of handing the insignia of the KBE to Gerry Wagner and never expecting to see tears in the eyes of the Chairman of Royal Dutch/Shell.

Dutch, incidentally, is almost as difficult a language as Hebrew. Indeed, they have in common the characteristic that, to pronounce them both, one must fill one's mouth with 'h's and gargle. But unlike Hebrew there is little credit to be gained by trying to speak Dutch. One must read it, of course, But if you try to speak it they either answer in faultless English or break into such rapid Dutch that you cannot understand a word or, more likely, they just laugh at your accent. So it is safer to stick to English, which they all speak beautifully.

Travel in Holland is as rewarding as in Israel, with a museum in almost every town and generous Dutchmen offering boat-trips across the Ijsselmeer, the former Zuider Zee. But it was much easier than in Israel to drive across frontiers. Many Dutchmen spend their holidays in the Dordogne and one summer we followed their example, poised happily between the vineyards of Bordeaux and the caves of prehistoric man. We visited both, being right royally received at several châteaux thanks largely to kind introductions by Cyril Ray and the hospitality of Max Joseph. But the highlight of that summer was undoubtedly a visit to Lascaux. Having had a father passionately and even controversially dedicated to the idea of evolution, I had wanted to visit these caves with their primitive wall-drawings for many years. But soon after the Second World War they had been closed to the public, when it was realised that visitors' breath was gradually obliterating the paintings. However, after some months of string-pulling we had managed to obtain a permit to visit. We were told on pain of death that we must arrive at a fixed time, no sooner or later, that we must wear rubber soles several inches thick with our toes covered, that no one under the age of fifteen would be admitted and that, once inside, we should barely breathe and certainly not talk. Needless to say, we arrived late, we only wore ordinary shoes, we were accompanied by a ten-year-old son and being late we were panting for breath. So we gave our son an ice-cream to console him for being left behind and made for the entrance. They could not have been more welcoming and even told us to bring the boy; never have I seen him throw away an ice-cream before or since. We were taken round by a guide, who, thirty years before, had been one of the boys who had discovered the caves while playing with a ball in the fields above.

The Lascaux paintings are superb, one sees them in complete freedom and thanks one's lucky stars that never again will one have to scrape one's scalp crouching through less spacious subterranean caves. Nothing else could ever match these. Our fellow visitor, incidentally, was the Belgian Minister of Education, called De Croo, who felt sure that he was directly descended from Cro-magnon man. Only one doubt remained: the Japanese were understood to be constructing an exact replica of Lascaux inside the next hill, tourists for the use of. We are satisfied that we saw the original.

For another holiday we had planned to go to Crete. But shortly before we were due to leave there was a bomb incident at Athens airport, through which we had to travel. Not wanting to expose three children to these hazards, we switched destination at short notice to Tunisia, where we found ourselves in a Club Mediterranée encampment on the sea-shore. We had our little villa and could cater for ourselves or could patronise the communal centre, where *animateurs* made sure that we enjoyed ourselves. Each Wednesday evening the entertainment consisted of the *me'schoui*: we started by hacking with knives at whole, vast sheep lying across the table. After dinner came the entertainment: horses doing *haute école* on the dance floor, followed by the snake charmers. My neighbour was dragged into the arena and had a live snake wound round his head. Not relishing this, I crouched back in my chair, hoping to avoid detection. No such luck. I was pulled forward, and laid flat with my head touching the ground. While I was congratulating myself that they could not tie a snake round my head in this position, they suddenly passed a live snake from top to bottom underneath my trousers. Had I known what was going to happen, I should have swum the Mediterranean. It all took place so quickly that my wife could not even snap a photograph.

When with the passage of years the time came to return to private life, we unwisely chose to leave Holland on Friday the 13th of May. It proved an ill-omened day indeed. When the Chief of Protocol came to say goodbye on behalf of the Foreign Minister and I raised my glass to toast him and Holland generally, one of my teeth promptly fell out into the glass. We then set off in two cars, both loaded to the gunwhales with cases of drink which we hoped we could personally negotiate through the English customs. My wife was driving in front, when to my horror I saw her car swaying from side to side, hitting a lorry and ending up against the central barrier of the motorway. A tyre had burst. Luckily, my wife came to no harm, but the car was a write-off and we had to leave several cases of precious liquor at the roadside. No doubt it was a judgement on greed.

We had had five very agreeable years and my advice to any budding diplomat would certainly be: 'Don't be vague. Ask for The Hague.'

10
Small Talk at Hurstpierpoint
WITH APOLOGIES TO CECIL TORR OF WREYLAND

Hurst is the equivalent of the German word *'Forst'* for forest. Thus Hurstpierpoint was the piece of forest given by William the Conqueror to Mr Pierpoint. Similarly, along the road, Herstmonceaux was Mr Monceux' share of the forest. This may sound fanciful, but at Falaise, from where the Conqueror set out, is a plaque on the drawbridge wall listing the knights who accompanied him. Sure enough, among them are Robert de Pierpoint and Guillaume de Monceux. So far, so good. But what of Billingshurst? It is hard to believe that Mr Billings came over with the Conqueror. It has been suggested that, once the knights were satisfied, a chunk of forest was made over to the villeins, who were corrupted into billings. Another theory is that Billings derives from William's own name and that this is a part of the forest which he kept for himself. But also, I discovered lately, in the age of migrations there was a movement in the Baltic area called the March of the Bullings. Could they also have done an about-turn and marched into England, converting from Bullings into Billings on the way?

Our house, Hampton Lodge, dates from the reign of William IV and the original design is attributed to Amon Wilds, much of whose work is to be found in Brighton. His trademark is a capital, to a pillar or a pilaster, shaped like an ammonite shell fossil and thus recalling the designer's first name. But the house has suffered many alterations and enlargements in the intervening years. We bought it in 1953 as a home for my father in his retirement. But, alas, he only lived for six months and could not enjoy it. My mother lived on in the house for ten more years and made it a welcoming home for the children and ourselves, especially while we were abroad.

My mother was a lynchpin of the family for many years. For my father, she had not only maintained the infrastructure of his life; she had ably supported him in his actual work too, sharing most of his political and religious attitudes. In the dedication of one of his books, he called her 'the best and severest of critics'. For the rest of us, she was an ever-present help, and not only in time of trouble. Her family, forbears, collaterals and descendants, meant a great deal to her and she had an encyclopaedic knowledge of all its ramifications. With many of its members, and especially of course with her own two sons, she kept in constant touch by letters in her beautiful handwriting and she took an infinity of trouble over Christmas and birthday presents. Her own possessions meant more to her for their associations, with people she had known and cared for, than for their intrinsic value or beauty. Indeed, she had an almost animistic affection for objects with which she was surrounded, called them by the names of their former owners. But, apart from her deep devotion to my father's memory, she remained to the end of her days more interested in the living than in the dead and we all knew that we could always rely on her abiding interest and love; and, if that makes her sound dull, it does no justice to her sharp critical faculty and her ironic sense of humour. As a young woman she had been an accomplished amateur actress and through her life she played her various parts to perfection. I cannot really write about her with detachment.

We ourselves have lived in this house for two main periods: when I was working in London in the 1960s and again since retirement in 1977. So our children have essentially been brought up at Hampton Lodge. Indeed, when we had our fifth child in 1964, we decided that family holidays in hotels were no longer desirable. Children in hotels, especially in large numbers, create misery for themselves, for their parents and for all their fellow guests. So we built a swimming-pool in the garden and decided that that could be the future focus for their summer holidays. Apart from the occasional intruders, including one night when Cynthia surprised eight naked youths and eight naked girls all bathing together, it has served its purpose well.

Swimming pools can be hazards. I was told of the time when the English College at Rome built a new pool and invited the local English Cardinal to open it. They expected him just to pronounce a blessing. But no, bald as he was, he stripped off his scarlet cassock, revealing an antique pair of shorts, from which the elastic had long since departed, and plunged in. While he was under the water, his shorts parted company from him and he re-emerged, as they say in the wine trade, bottoms up, whereupon the rector of the College was heard to exclaim, 'Good Lord, he's split his head open.'

Nowadays, of course, our house is far too big for Darby and Joan. But we have spent too much of our life moving around the world to want the self-inflicted injury of yet another move. What is more, the house is practically held up by books and we should be miserable without them, so that if we did move we should need almost as large a house to accommodate the books. Even though many of my grandfather's books went to form the Ward Library at Peterhouse and my father's theological library was presented to Exeter University, we still seem to have inherited hundreds of volumes from each of them, quite apart from those which we have been unable to resist acquiring ourselves. In theory there is no longer any shelf-space for books or wall-space for shelves. But still they seem to accumulate. My parents' generation seems to have preserved things: our own seems more inclined to acquire things. The end result in both cases tends to be congestion.

If a house is a machine to live in, Cynthia must be an expert mechanic. She has kept both house and garden working like clockwork during all our years here, storms, subsidence and other alarms and excursions notwithstanding. Most of it has been her own unaided physical work. No doubt the genes help. Her mother was an indefatigable housekeeper and her father must have had green fingers, having run agriculture in India and then, for the last twenty-five years of his life, on half an acre in Bournemouth. Cynthia herself seems to have discovered the secret of eternal youth, which is only one of the many things about her for which I am intensely grateful.

In the garden she has had stalwart support from Fenner, our part-time gardener. He has been coming to us for twenty-five years and is still doing so in his early nineties, still with the energy of a man twenty-five years younger. We do not ask whether his loyalty is primarily to us or to the garden; whichever it is, we are enormously in his debt. Not that he was originally a gardener by trade; until he retired he was an electrician and to this day one can hardly squeeze into his house for the mass of electric equipment it contains. He is a ham radio-operator and we understand that at night he is in frequent communication with King Hussein of Jordan, who is a fellow-practitioner.

My first task on retirement was to write my father's life. Not liking any of the volunteer would-be biographers, I had kept his papers to myself and, as a result of this dog-in-the-manger attitude, felt that I now must write the book, even though it is probably unwise for a son to write about his father, steering an uneasy course between excessive filial piety and indecorous criticism. It would have been better if the book had been written and published twenty-five years earlier, when there were still plenty of people around who were familiar with my father himself and the activities and ideas in which he was involved. But luckily, armed with his papers and the press-cuttings which my mother had assiduously collected, I did not have too hard a task. There were not so many people left to interview or interrogate, but those who remained were consistently helpful, as were librarians at Birmingham, Cambridge and Lambeth. I was able to consult official archives, some of them not open to the public, and Collins proved extremely cooperative publishers. Above all, Victor Rothschild most generously arranged for me to have house-room, with the full-time services of a secretary in the bank's headquarters at New Court. Victor had a reputation for a certain rudeness, but, in fact, he was a very kind man, almost to a fault. Thanks to these kindnesses I was able to complete the job in two years and it was published in 1979 under the title *Ahead of His Age*.

The book brought me my one and only television appearance, when I was asked to talk about it to Hugh Montefiore, the then Bishop of Birmingham. He challenged me by saying that my father did not have a strong pastoral dimension. I wish now that I had had the presence of mind to tell him that my father had more than once gone to visit prisoners in the condemned cell at their request and to give them what comfort he could. If that is not pastoral, what is?

Soon I found myself doing odd jobs in the City of London, the County of Sussex and the Church of England, which provided enough variety to keep me busy and interested. In the City, apart from two or three non-executive directorships, I inaugurated the scholarship scheme for the children of Rothschild executives at independent schools. The bank had set up a fund to finance some twenty scholarships every year. We arranged for Westminster School to set and mark the papers and I assembled a committee of ex-headmasters and a headmistress, as statutory woman, to interview the successful candidates. It was hard work, with a dozen or more children coming into the room at intervals of fifteen minutes, so that one had to discover what made each child tick, then actually make it tick and finally ease it out of the room on time with no tears shed. One of my colleagues regularly asked 'What would you do if you were suddenly given £100?'

This never worked. Either the child of a merchant banker obviously regarded £100 as chicken feed, too trivial to worry about, or answered virtuously, 'I should put it in the bank.' But in the course of eleven years we met some lively candidates too, many of whom are already in good jobs, and of course the scheme continues in other hands.

These and other activities in London have been made much easier by having a pied-à-terre there, thanks to the generosity of Ian Anstruther. We have known each other since 1946 in Washington, where he was attached to Archie Inverchapel; we are godfathers to each other's children, I am a trustee of some of his family's trusts, as now are two of our children, and in London I perch on his family estate. It is a friendship which has meant a great deal to us all.

My Church of England jobs have been described elsewhere. In civil life in Sussex my main commitments were to serve on the Council of Sussex University, as chairman of the Governors of Hurstpierpoint College and as chairman of the Sussex Rural Community Council. With the blood of Dr Arnold's sister flowing in my veins, I suppose I was fated to take an interest in schools. Education had of course changed out of all recognition since I was at school. We had lived in more or less monastic establishments, where one never saw a girl from beginning to end of the term. Nor did we ever spent a night away from school. Now half-term seems to last for ten days and almost every weekend is spent at home. Nor, to judge from the posters and other artwork in boys' study-bedrooms, do they have much left to learn about pretty girls. But Hurstpierpoint College remained an all-boys boarding school, a preserve of male chauvinist pigs, if you like. As a member of the Southern Division of the Woodard Schools, it belonged to a group which included one school with girls only in the sixth form (Lancing), one with girls mixing all through (Ardingly) and one for girls only (St Michael's Petworth). So there was plenty of parental choice and at Hurstpierpoint we found no difficulty in filling the school from those parents who deliberately preferred an all-male education. Fewer distractions, presumably.

Our family has not spurned female education, let me hasten to say. All three of our daughters went to Wycombe Abbey, where my grandfather had been a founding governor, my mother was a governor for many years, my brother followed and became chairman of the governors and our daughter Sarah is now a governor.

Rural Community Councils, of which there is one in every county under that or a similar name, are not just exercises in conservation. On the contrary, as the name implies, they are involved with the communities themselves rather than with their environment. We were concerned with people, not with things. We were not abominable no-men, resisting all development. We welcomed anything which could contribute to the prosperity of rural Sussex, although we would hope that it could be achieved with minimal adverse effect on local amenities. On the whole, it was an uphill task. Sussex-on-the-Sea tended to be the mecca for businesmen from the Midlands retiring with golden handshakes, who forced up the price of property in our villages, so that old people retiring from tied cottages, or young couples wanting to marry, could not afford to buy homes in their own villages but were forced into the big coastal towns, where they tended to swell the ranks of the unemployed. Thus many of the much-publicised defects of the inner cities in fact originated in the problems of the countryside. To make matters worse, if there were no young couples and thus no children in a village, the village school might be closed; if mothers were not bringing their children to school, there would not be enough customers to support a village shop; if no one came to shop, the bus service might be removed, there would not be enough business for a sub-post office and so on down and round the vicious circle. Villages were dying on the vine, especially as many of the northern immigrants took little practical interest in their new surroundings or their new neighbours. These difficulties are not peculiar to Sussex; but in the South East we were living in an area where prices, particularly of property, were well above the national average and wages, which were predominantly agricultural, well below it. In trying to reverse these processes, we were brought into close touch with local government, particularly on the planning side, and this was for me a new interest and a new dimension.

For, unless Rural Community Council enters into a relationship with its County Council to act as its agent for specific purposes, it disposes of no funds to conduct operations on its own account. Such resources as it has, coming from the Rural Development Commission or from its own fund-raising efforts, are essentially used on its own administrative expenses or on promotional activities, conferences and the like to persuade other people to do things, in fields such as housing, transport, employment or community care. It is in fact a mixture of a gnat and a midwife: a gnat on the rump of the statutory authorities who have the power to make things happen and a midwife to induce rural communities to help themselves and to articulate their own needs. In all this, the church, notably its Board of Social Responsibility, was a useful ally, as was the university, with its research facilities covering local information. So having links with both those bodies, one was in a position to facilitate a certain amount of cross-fertilisation.

Cynthia meanwhile, apart from being an active hostess and housekeeper, and interesting herself in our own village conservation society, soon became a magistrate and has found this work intensely rewarding. I tell her that the more she does it, the more I sympathise with the malefactors. My own contacts with the Law started badly. At Winchester we were, in our last year, allowed to attend the assize court, usually for some petty larceny case. On my first day there we were shown into the courtroom. Soon afterwards the jury filed into the box, the judge appeared on the bench, a prisoner was ushered into the dock and the clerk rose to ask 'Gentlemen of the jury, what is your verdict?' 'Guilty, my lord, of murder', and before we knew where we were, the judge had the black cap on and was delivering all the ghastly rigmarole of the death sentence. The murderer was known to the press as 'the man with the glaring eyes' who had run down young women at night in his car; I think he was later reprieved.

At Trinity the judge on assize was put up in the Master's Lodge and I was once invited to dine with one of them, Mr Justice du Parcq, who had known my father at the Temple. The marshal's note read: 'The judge says you need not wear knee breeches.' This was just as well, as never in my wildest dreams would it have occurred to me to put on knee breeches, even if I had possessed them.

On the subject of knee breeches, there was a story told at that time of a high sheriff who thought he could make do with the court dress which he had worn twenty years earlier and was now distinctly too tight for him. At the assize service, next to Mr Justice Horridge, he thought the most he could manage was to lean forward to pray. Horridge turned on him: 'Kneel down, sir, kneel down in the house of God.' He had to obey, but his breeches split irrevocably in sight of the whole congregation. Determined to have his revenge, he staged a party with Horridge as principal guest and engaged an entertainer, popular in London in those days, who specialised in removing your braces without your knowledge. Horridge's trousers came down and honour was satisfied.

A barrister friend of mine was once engaged in a case in which all the parties were from Chinatown. Apparently the Chinese took the oath either by wringing the neck of a cockerel or by breaking a saucer. The judge ruled that no cockerels' necks were to be wrung in his court. So by the end of the case policemen in hobnailed boots advanced to the witness box crunching broken china beneath their feet. Meanwhile, whenever a Chinese witness launched into a long and excited high-pitched declamation, the interpreter merely contributed 'He says "No".' It reminded me of a fellow undergraduate at Trinity from Malaya called Ng. The praelector decided that, when he had to name him in a roll-call, he would just twang a tuning-fork once.

Another of Cynthia's retirement activities has been with the Order of St John, first with the Ladies' Guild supporting the Ophthalmic Hospital in Jerusalem and then as a member, and eventually chairman, of the Council of St John Ambulance for Sussex. This has involved her in a great deal of successful fund-raising and has also led to her appointment as a Sister of St John, which makes me feel that I must be a son-in-law of Zebedee.

One of the pleasures of retirement was to consist of watching cricket. Thanks to Harold Caccia, I was already a member of MCC. Now I became a life-member of Sussex County Cricket Club, having found by experience that it pays hand over fist to take out life membership of any institution if one can. This was no exception, to judge by what I paid in 1977 compared with what one would have to pay now. So I have had many happy days at Lord's and Hove cricket grounds. I had watched cricket with my mother from an early age, often at Taunton and once memorably at an England v. Australia Test Match at Trent Bridge in 1938, with Bradman, McCabe and others scoring prolifically. My mother was very noble in accompanying me, but slightly embarrassing in that, every time a batsman hit a boundary, she shouted 'Good ball.'

Cynthia too had to be introduced to cricket. She and I were to witness Bradman's last innings in Test cricket at the Oval in 1948. When he came in, we were all on our feet cheering. There were tears in every eye, no doubt in Bradman's too. He missed Hollies's first ball and was bowled by the second. We were all on our feet cheering and weeping again.

Fortified by this experience, my dear wife was once explaining the finer points of cricket to a French boy staying with us on an exchange visit. She told him, to arouse his interest, of a gardener's boy we had once employed who, playing village cricket at a weekend, had bowled a ball which the batsman hit firmly to square leg, killing the umpire there. When we later took the French boy to Hove cricket ground, he surveyed the scene eagerly, asking 'Où sont les morts?'

Sometimes I watched cricket from the committee room at Edgbaston where my Uncle Stanley was President of Warwickshire C.C.C. He left a generous legacy to build what is still known as the Stanley Barnes stand. My father had three brothers, one of whom, Uncle Alfred, died quite young as a civil servant during the First World War. Stanley, a neurologist, became the senior physician at Birmingham General Hospital and then, as dean of the university's medical school, was the leading figure in building the Queen Elizabeth Hospital, then the very model of a modern major hospital. He was also a shrewd investor and used to say that, when the Labour Government came into power in 1924, he had sold every share he possessed; when it fell less than a year later, he bought back in again and doubled his capital. He was a strong Conservative and, though publicly absolutely loyal to his family, was inclined to wonder in private whether his own chances, of a knighthood for example, had not been damaged by association with his notorious brother, the radical bishop. The youngest brother, Sidney, did become knighted, as Deputy Secretary of the Admiralty. In that capacity, he was responsible for building the wartime addition to the Admiralty, the vast brick iceberg known to the public as the Citadel, but to my uncle as 'my little wooden hut'. Before the First War he had been private secretary to Prince Louis of Battenberg as First Sea Lord, so that, when in the Second War he visited Lord Mountbatten in South-East Asia, he did not know whether to address him as 'my dear young man' or 'Supreme Commander, sir'. He later became Director of Greenwich Hospital and was for a time chairman of the United University Club, where he used to regale us with a splendid drink called a Double Blue, with a base of blue curaçao.

Without wishing to appear addicted to alcohol, I must in all honesty declare an interest. Perhaps it started young. When I dined with my housemaster at Winchester, his butler used to bend low and mutter in one's ear a long litany of which the only intelligible part was the end '... cider, lemonade or water, sir?' One longed to sample the forbidden fruits which had gone before. My housemaster, Monty

Wright, once a pupil of my father at Trinity, was known as the Second Master and when, during my time there, he decided to marry, he told us 'It will be very nice to have a second mistress.'

When we went to Beirut in 1952, we sailed in a Norwegian cargo boat, with the whole family and all our worldly goods on board, including a new car. Those were the days when diplomats moving abroad could still take with them the entire contents of a house. We took three tons, and eventually moved into an unfurnished flat on the Rue el Hamra. During the rougher passages of the journey we could hear something rolling with ominous sounds from side to side of the hold. The captain told us that it was our car. In fact, when we reached Kalamata in Southern Greece, they unloaded some large empty oil-drums. We were told that when the ship came back in three weeks' time, they would collect these drums, by then filled with Greek grape-juice and a chemical to stop it fermenting. On return to England they would deliver the drums to a well-known cider firm, who would put in another chemical to make the liquid ferment in double-quick time, bottle it and sell it as 'British wine'. It did not sound very appetising and is not to be confused with English wine, grown on English vineyards and prepared in accordance with proper principles of vinification. One of the best English vineyards is at Beaulieu and once, when Edward Montagu came to stay at The Hague, he brought us two bottles of Beaulieu '73 and told us to wrap them in a napkin, serve them to the French Ambassador and ask him what he thought they were. The Frenchman, to his eternal credit, sniffed, sipped, tasted and asked 'Could this be a Chablis?' Diplomacy at its best.

Some months after we arrived in Germany in 1953, we were taken on a wine-tasting expedition to Wehlen on the Mosel. 1953 had been a great year and we carried home several cases of Wehlener Sonnenuhr '53. When we were leaving Bonn in 1958 we went back to the same firm and asked for some more of the '53. Thinking us strangers, they said that it was sold out, but that we could have the '55, nothing like such a good year. So we sat down and asked after the sister's arthritis and the nephew who had fallen out of a tree, and so on and so on. After half an hour of these reminiscences, the penny dropped and we came away with a plentiful supply of the '53.

Enough of alcoholism. My favourite drink story is of the New Yorker who went into a bar and ordered twelve martinis. When they were set up on the bar, he threw the left-hand glass over his left shoulder and the right-hand glass over his right shoulder. The barman expostulated: 'You asked for twelve and now you only have ten.' 'Oh yes, but the first one tastes so nasty and the last one makes you tight.'

During our spell at home in the 1960s, when we thought our family was complete and before we decided to build a swimming-pool, we had ourselves painted in a conversation piece by John (professionally know as William) Dring. As he was an Academician, we thought he would be too expensive for us; but he said he was so tired of painting gents' natty suitings for boardroom portraits, or university gowns for college halls, that he would meet our price. He came to stay for a few days to inspect us and then returned in the school holidays with an oil sketch outlining us all in the colours he wanted. We each sat individually for our place in the picture. By the weekend when I returned from London, five portraits were almost complete. I then had to sit with my arm stretched out like an Indian fakir for two hours or more; but Dring regaled me with so many scurrilous stories that it was only when I was released that I realised I could no longer bend the arm. The only trouble about that picture was that, when our fifth child arrived later, we could not fit him in, except perhaps in a pram on the lawn or as a bubble arising from one of our heads. Some years later he graduated to a portrait on his own, by our dear friend Sybil Richardson, wife of the distinguished doctor, who painted under the name Sybil Trist. We are also in her debt for a delightful portrait of Cynthia.

Over the years we have picked up a few other pictures, mostly drawings or watercolours in the days when they were affordable and also some works by my Lancaster forebears, no connection with either Osbert or John of Gaunt. My great-great-grandfather, Richard Hume Lancaster, was a clergyman who used to exhibit at the Royal Academy until it was suggested to him that it was improper for a parson to paint for profit. The art historians often confuse him with his son Hume: their names were very similar, as were some of the subjects which they painted, and the son died, in fact, before the father. The son, by general agreement, was the better artist but, from all appearances, a less respectable citizen, although he too regularly exhibited at the Academy for most of his life. Their works are to be found in several public galleries, including the Tate, and in the Government collection lent out to embassies and so on.

Other exercises in picture-buying included a time when we saw a drawing advertised at Christie's as by 'J. Constable, R.A.', a form of description which usually implies that the auctioneer thinks it may be authentic. So my wife went to bid and secured it for three guineas. Greatly elated, we treated ourselves to an excellent luncheon at Prunier's and took our prize to Agnew's, where a very supercilious character told us 'If you want a formal opinion, I shall have to lay it before the directors and charge you a fee; but if that is the drawing which was sold at Christie's this morning as a Constable, I can tell you that you do not get a Constable for three guineas.' We retired in disorder, but it is a nice drawing.

Another time I went to the first London exhibition of David Hockney and Patrick Procktor. Needless to say, I decided to buy a Procktor, which is an attractive picture but not an investment in the Hockney class. Or once when I was asked by the Yugoslav Embassy to an exhibition of Yugoslav pictures and it was clear that I should not be allowed out of the place without buying a picture, I took one by an artist called Feyes, who was reported to work in a coalmine and come up once a week to paint pictures from postcards. When in Belgrade a little later I proudly recounted my purchase, only to be told 'There are six originals of every Feyes.'

Luckily we no longer have any wall space for pictures. So economy is enforced upon us.

But we did have one stroke of luck. My great-uncle John Ward had married the daughter of Baron von Gerolt, then Prussian Minister at Washington. In the Napoleonic Wars I am afraid that the Gerolts must have been collaborators with the French invaders and one of them became Minister-President of the Confederation of the Rhine. So, when Uncle John's daughter died at a great age in the 1950s we found among her papers two letters of appointment signed 'Bonaparte', one of them also counter-signed by Talleyrand.

I have in fact had several lucky breaks. Once in a deserted street off Piccadilly in about 1980 I picked up a bundle of banknotes, which I virtuously took to the nearest police station. I was told to leave them for a month and, if they were then not claimed, I could have them. A month later they turned out to amount to £65 and I was able to buy Cynthia quite a good dinner.

Another time, we flew from Tel Aviv to stay with friends, Harry and Ruth Kosin, in the south of France. After dinner they insisted on going to the casino at Cannes, where they went off to play baccarat, which I do not understand. So I watched the roulette table, which is a simple process. When hours later Cynthia came to say it was time to go home, I insisted, over her protests, on making just one bet and put 100 french francs on the date of my birthday. It came up *en plein*, 36 to 1, and, in less time than it takes to tell, I had won our air fares from Tel Aviv to Nice and back. I treated myself to one glass of Coca-Cola and we went home.

Luckiest of all, perhaps, I had been telling Cynthia that if you go to a show of pictures, you must buy the catalogue or you will not remember what you have seen. She was protesting that we had no spare shelves to house them. Next day I found myself at a small exhibition of Florentine pictures with a rather expensive catalogue. Nevertheless I felt in duty bound to buy it. When reaching home that evening, I opened it and out fell a piece of paper: 'This is the lucky catalogue. You have won a week's holiday for two people in Florence.' To our eternal shame we accepted the offer and had a wonderful week, visiting not only Florence but Siena, San Gimignano, Livorno and Ravenna.

We had some other good holidays during the 1960s. In 1960 itself we went to Oberammergau to see the Passion Play. My grandfather had visited it nearly one hundred years earlier in 1871, when the play had been postponed for a year on account of the Franco-Prussian war. We ourselves had been to Oberammergau out of season, while we lived at Bonn. It was strange to go into one dressing-room and see six crowns of thorns hanging on pegs on the wall. There were other incongruities when we watched the play itself. A jet aircraft flew across the back of the open stage while the Last Supper was in progress in front of it. When Judas entered to hang himself, a thunderstorm broke. Rain stopped play and he had to roll up his rope and march off stage, until weather permitted him to come back and finish the job. But for all that it was a really moving spectacle and the much criticised anti-semitism, which in any case derives more from medieval monks than from twentieth-century Nazis, was hardly noticeable.

Another year, after a particularly harsh English winter, we decided to escape for a week to Marrakech, to the Hotel Mamounia. It is a wonderful oasis in the desert of Morocco, with the snow-capped Atlas mountains in the distance, where one could have skied if one wanted. As it was, we fed the birds from our balcony and bathed in the pool, out of which palm trees were growing, or went to watch the gathering of carpet merchants, water-sellers and snake charmers of an evening in the vast market place. On the way to Marrakech we had stopped for a night at Casablanca, where Cynthia suddenly announced that she had never seen a belly dance. I appealed to the hall porter, who told us to take the first turn to the right, the second to the left and go through the bead curtain under the red light. We found ourselves a table in an obscure corner and sat patiently awaiting the floor show. But the proprietor descended upon us and dragged us on to the stage. Next we knew, only four hours from London Airport, we were not watching the belly dance, but performing it ourselves.

I have always wanted to take Cynthia on a Hellenic cruise, as my parents had taken me twice in the 1930s. Sir Henry Lunn, the founder and proprietor of the Hellenic Travellers Club, was generous to a fault. My father was given a free passage in exchange for one lecture on each cruise and my mother and I received substantial reductions. In those far-off days my fare for fourteen days on board, plus all the excursions, amounted to £15. It was not surprising that from time to time Henry Lunn had to come to an arrangement with his creditors. But the organisation was excellent, the company was pretty distinguished and we really saw Greece, with learned lectures every few footsteps. On one of these cruises we embarked at Marseilles and my father made me the courier for our drive across France. There came the day when we broke the main leaf of the rear spring of the car and I was sent off to have it mended. Being ignorant of all machinery, I consulted the dictionary: spring = ressort, main leaf = *maîtresse*. So, aged seventeen, I strode into the garage and announced: 'Bonjour. J'ai cassé ma maîtresse.' The effect was electric.

On the subject of the French language, Sammy Hood, who was one of the best bosses for whom I ever worked, used to tell the story of an occasion in the Second War when de Gaulle called on Churchill in Downing Street. Relations were rather strained at the time and the private secretaries waited apprehensively in the outer office in case the great men came to blows. At last Winston's head came round the door and he asked 'What is the opposite of "Vive la France"?'

Private secretaries have a difficult life. The story was told of a visitor to Buckingham Palace walking along a corridor and through an open door hearing a deep masculine voice declaring 'and, of course, we women . . .' This was Jock Colville dictating a draft speech for the then Princess Elizabeth, to whom he was at the time private secretary.

Another chief I much admired was Derick Hoyer-Millar, later Lord Inchyra. He was the most deceptively amateur professional and an extremely professional amateur. Even as head of the Foreign Office he usually knew more about the business of one's department than one did oneself; and, like the Duke of Wellington, he attached real importance to looking after 'the common soldiers committeed to his charge', in this case those of us who served on his staff.

Derick was immensely generous in involving younger members of his Embassy in interesting occasions. Well do I remember one luncheon where General Montgomery was the guest of honour. There was among the other guests the French General Beauffre, anxious above all to justify his country's performance at Dien Bien Phu. There was General Heusinger, head of the renascent German Army, determined to discover which battle-tank he ought to be buying. Monty would have none of this and kept repeating that one must win the air battle before one started on the land battle, that before one started the land battle one must win the air battle, and so on in his inimitable repetitive style. He must incidentally be performing contortions in his grave to pat himself on the back for the immense success with which his doctrine was applied in the Gulf War.

I suppose the young always react well to kindness from their elders, and so they should. In 1936 I was one of a small party invited over from Winchester to Eton for the Fourth of June. We were asked to luncheon by the Provost, who was Monty James; he came to table with the Order of Merit round his neck. Poor man, he only had ten more days to live. At the other end of the table I found myself sitting next to the fabled Lady Desborough, who should have been well above the salt. Having been a *grande dame* of the Edwardian era, she was cruelly satirised by Max Beerbohn, but nothing could have exceeded the unaffected charm with which she entertained a callow teenaged schoolboy.

This I remembered years later when I sat next at dinner to Violet Bonham-Carter. Lady Violet had had a fearsome reputation as a member of the board interviewing young candidates for the Foreign Office. But she was an extremely entertaining neighbour, telling a story of Maurice Baring who, having stayed the weekend with the Desboroughs at Panshanger, was writing his bread and butter letter, or 'Collins' as he would probably have called it, from London: 'Dear Lady Desborough, That was a most delightful Saturday to Monday and I am writing to thank you as I listen to this new-fangled device, the wireless. But to my horror I have just heard on it that Lord Desborough is dead. This is terrible as he was in such excellent form only at luncheon today. What can I say? Oh, it's all right. It's Lord Bessborough after all. Yours ever, Maurice Baring.'

These snobbish reflections remind me that as a boy I used to collect autographs. Not only did I hang around cricket grounds, pestering the players with my little book. In 1930 a fellow-Dragon and I were presented with the signatures of the whole Australian touring team. We tossed up to see who would have first pick. Needless to say, he won and took Bradman. I was also much indebted to my father, who very nobly used to badger his neighbours at dinners and meetings on my behalf. In this way, among others, I acquired Gandhi, Marconi, Baldwin, Tagore (in Hindi), Einstein, Rutherford and Bernard Shaw.

Another legacy from my father lay in my insurance policy. As a tutor at Trinity in the early years of the century he used to leave in his pupils' waiting-room the brochures of his insurance company, the Fine Art & General. On the strength of this he became an agent of the company and, in due course, I inherited his agency, which after various takeovers and mergers, had passed to the Commercial Union. To this day I am allowed to deduct a percentage from every premium. Indeed, the Commercial Union have been extremely generous to us. When our house here at Hurstpierpoint showed signs of subsidence at one corner, they undertook responsibility for curing it, as they have done for the extensive damage caused to the roof by the storms of October 1987 and January 1990. We are very grateful to them.

My father had other experiences as a Cambridge tutor. One of his pupils was a nephew of Pobedonostsev, Procurator of the Holy Synod in Russia and an official of a fearsome reputation. The young man got into some sort of scrape from which my father rescued him. As a thank offering the Procurator sent him two cases of Imperial Tokay, of which a single bottle still remained in our Hurstpierpoint cellar in 1990. According to Raymond Postgate, it has the useful property of reviving you on your deathbed.

Another pupil came to my father to say that he had met a charming group of people with whom he wanted to spend a weekend retreat, with a view to ordination. My father, being in orders himself, did not feel he could refuse him leave, and off he went. Shortly afterwards the young man had his twenty-first birthday, on which day a gang of obvious crooks, attended by an obnoxious clergyman in the guise of chaplain, appeared in my father's room to claim that the boy had signed over all his property to them. My father, in some alarm, approached the young man's guardian, who announced with glee that his ward did not come into his inheritance until he was twenty-five, so that the gang had shown their hand too early and their knavish tricks were frustrated. Some thirty years later my father had to sit as an assessor on a consistory court trying the notorious Davidson, rector of Stiffkey. He was much intrigued, but not too surprised, to recognise the defendant as the chaplain of that gang all those years before.

My own undergraduate experiences were less dramatic. I was still spending vacations in France and Germany trying to learn the languages. In Paris my hostess, Contesse de Dormy, used to take me almost daily to play bridge in the Quartier St Germain, usually at the *hôtel particulier* of the dear old Princesse du Scey, where all the men were generals and all the women at least countesses, including Mme de Corday, of the same family as the murderess of Marat, who always said that she liked her tea 'comme le pipi des colombes'. But the only drink not served at those gatherings was tea. My bridge was bad enough at any time. But after lashings of port at 4 p.m., it deteriorated sharply and I lost heavily. No one showed any sympathy, the pound was strong and 'il joue avec des livres'. Luckily, my father paid my gaming debts in the interests of learning French.

In Munich my visits coincided with the opera season: Mozart at the little rococo Residenztheater, Wagner at the massive Prinzregententheater and Strauss at the classical Nationaltheater. We students had a separate queue and a quarter of an hour before the curtain rose we were allotted all the unsold tickets at Reichsmarks 4.50 each, then about 4/6d. One would find oneself sitting in *Lederhosen* or in dirty grey flannels in the second row of the stalls, next to some pompous and disapproving German in white tie and tails.

Back in Cambridge, we were more balletomanes than opera buffs, as Maynard Keynes and Lydia Lopokova brought the Vic-Wells Ballet regularly to the Arts Theatre. A high point was to find myself in Margot Fonteyn's dressing-room, as she washed her hair after a performance, peeping out from under her tresses with that elfin look of hers. Years later Rudolf Nureyev came to supper after the theatre to our house at The Hague. He was dehydrated after dancing and we tried to restore him with beakers of white wine and soda water. He seemed pleased to be treated as an Englishman in our Embassy, but when I said goodbye to him in all his winter furs, Russian-style, it was like being hugged by a grisly bear. Once at dinner Cynthia sat next to the Chairman of Covent

Gardens, Lord Drogheda, and told him how, at the age of eleven, ballerinas have their wrists measured to make sure that they are not going to grow too tall. She was astonished to find that he had never heard this before and he wrote afterwards to confirm that it was true.

Over the years one picks up strange bits of knowledge. As a boy I can remember Charles Grant Robertson, Vice-Chancellor of Birmingham University, coming to dinner at Bishop's Croft. His party trick as a historian was to enumerate all the people born in years ending in 9: Goethe 1749, Schiller 1759, Napoleon, Wellington, Castlereagh and Thomas Lawrence in 1769, Queen Victoria and the Prince Consort in 1819. But the vintage year was 1809 with Lincoln, Gladstone, Darwin, Tennyson, Mendelssohn, Braille and Edgar Allan Poe. My father had a simpler approach to historical dates. He remembered them by jingles: fourteen hundred and ninety two Columbus sailed the ocean blue; sixteen hundred and sixty-six London was burnt to rotten sticks; George the Third said with a smile seventeen sixty yards in a mile. Alexander the Great died in 323 B.C., between the ages of 32 and 33. My grandfather, who was a real historian, always said that he could never remember a date but was never more than two years out. Perhaps he would have found the jingles helpful.

Grant Robertson did not specialise in people who died in 9 years. One such was Captain Cook in 1779. Cynthia and I have been asked to several of the annual Ditchley Lectures and I have attended some Anglo-American conferences in the splendid and hospitable surroundings of Ditchley Park. At one conference Senator Fong of Hawaii was a speaker and introduced his remarks by saying that he was happy to be in England, as he always felt that he had a little bit of an Englishman in him, because his great-grandfather had eaten Captain Cook. After the meeting the wife of another Senator came up to him and, in all innocence and a baby-girl voice, asked him 'Senator Fong, is it really true that your great-grandfather ate Captain Cook?'

Heredity is a fascinating subject. It always seems to me that there are three vital stages in evolution: how did all things begin? How did life emerge? How did speech happen? The arrival of speech, the ability to communicate, is surely far more significant than the appearance on the scene of *homo erectus*, *homo habilis* or even *homo sapiens*. Even so, the most tragic figure in history must be the last ape whose son was the first man. Could anything be more humiliating? Now we are told that all humankind derives from a single woman in Africa. But if she was the first human, her mate must have been sub-human, another intolerable situation. One of the outstanding books of our generation is Jacques Monod's *Chance and Necessity*, by which he means that characteristics emerge by chance mutations but are then inherited by inevitable necessity. This brings to mind the dictum of my old chief, Ivone Kirkpatrick: 'Si on veut quelque chose, il faut en vouloir les conséquences'. But I am reluctant to subscribe to such a determinist philosophy. It is surely better to cling to Werner Heisenberg's 'uncertainty principle'. Although his theory derived from the unpredictable movement of particles, it surely has wide implications, moral, philosophical and even theological. It can be called in aid to explain the existence of evil under a benevolent deity or the presence of free will when God is omnipotent... As William Temple put it, 'God is limited by his material'.

I have said that I am allergic to machines, or perhaps they are allergic to me. But I have enjoyed travelling in a variety of machines, flying and otherwise. Hovercraft, helicopters and hydrofoils are now commonplace, although my first experience of a hydrofoil was in the Bay of Leningrad where, after a lavish luncheon with the mayor, the rush of air past the vessel was an excellent cure for a hangover. Concorde is now commonplace too, if you can afford it, which I cannot; but I did fly in a Concorde proving flight before it went into commerical service. On one anniversary of the Battle of Britain I flew round Holland in the cockpit of an aged Lancaster bomber, where the noise paralysed any attempt at coherent thought. But the two aircraft which were the most exciting were the Harrier and the Jaguar. In each case I was put into a flying suit and given careful instruction on how to eject: I hardly dared move my hands for fear of touching a button and soaring into the heavens. In the jump-jet Harrier, I was whirled round the sky and then we hovered in mid-air, with no visible means of support. In the Jaguar I sat behind Wing-Commander Sandy Wilson, who, as an Air Vice-Marshal, was to command our air forces in the Gulf in 1990. He allowed me for a time to take the controls and never have I felt so much power flowing from my fingertips.

Also in the field of technology, I have had to bear-lead official foreign visitors round the nuclear power centres at Harwell and Calder Hall, now Sellafield. These places are full of notices saying 'Beware of radiation'. I never knew what one was supposed to do: you cannot see it, hear it, smell it or feel it. In much the same way, what evasive action is one meant to take on the road if confronted with a sign 'Beware of low-flying aircraft'?

Nowadays life is much more tranquil and much of it devoted to reminiscence. If inside every fat man is a thin man trying to get out, so too inside every old man is a young man wanting to come back. This is neither the time nor the place to offer considered reflections on a life largely mis-spent in diplomacy, still less to write a diplomatic handbook. Indeed, it has always seemed to me that the principles on which diplomatic intercourse should be conducted are much the same as those which should govern normal, decent, human behaviour. It has been said that diplomacy is the ability to tell someone to go to hell and make him look forward to the journey. To put it more succinctly, more flies are caught by honey than by vinegar. To some extent all depends on being in the right place at the right time. It also depends on the ability to make the right contribution. As in so many walks of life, quality is more important than quantity. A few high-fliers adequately paid can contribute far more than a crowd of mediocrities looking over their shoulders to see where their next salary increase in coming from. That may sound selfish, or calculating, or ambitious. But I have always tried to preach, and I hope as far as possible practise what I have preached, that one should work for results rather than rewards. My father used to say that the only disqualification for a job was to ask for it. But, as Edmund Burke said, for evil to happen it is only necessary for good men to do nothing, even though Mandell Creighton also opined that no people do so much harm as those who go about doing good. Certainly, one should always try to think with the heart as well as with the head. Very often that will mean that, when confronted with a problem, one should ask oneself, not what one thinks about it, but what one should do about it. It also means, in diplomacy almost more than in other activities, one should try to put oneself in the other man's shoes and do as you would be done by. Time and again, this will also mean not asking either/or questions but looking for both/and answers. As the game theorists put it, neither diplomacy nor life should be a zero-sum game, in which one side takes all and the other nothing. It is a much better result if both sides leave the field content Surely, too, the contentment does not necessarily come from being acquisitive. The idea of service seems to have become totally unfashionable. Now everyone wants to make money. Have they forgotten what President Kennedy said in his inaugural address: 'Ask not what your country can do for you. Ask rather what you can do for your country'?

But these are quite enough pompous and sententious remarks to constitute a swan-song. Especially when looking back, one is inclined to echo Ovid: 'Video meliora proboque, deteriora sequor.'

Down the backstairs again.

Index

Acheson, Dean, 72-3, 99
Adenauer, Konrad, 96, 115-17
Adler, Barbara, 66, 67
Agagianian, Cardinal, 19
Alanbrooke, Field-Marshal Viscount, 52
Alexander of Tunis, Field-Marshal Earl, 73
Alfrink, Cardinal, 24, 25
Anstruther, Ian, 156
Appleton, Rt Rev George, 21
Attlee, Clement (Earl), 71, 73
Avon, Earl of, 60, 74, 117

Balfour, Sir John, 62
Ball, Rt Rev Peter, 30
Barnes, A. C. T. (mother), 10, 13, 32, 121, 122-3, 156
Barnes, Cynthia (Lady) (wife), 19, 20, 38, 39, 40, 90ff et passim
Barnes, Rt Rev E. W. (father), 10, 11, 13, 16, 18, 20, 30, 32, 33, 34, 35, 112, 120-1, 126, 152, 154-5, 158, 160, 165, 167-8, 171
Barnes, Jasper (son), 125, 131, 150, 153, 162
Barnes, Sir Sidney (uncle), 160
Barnes, Simon (son), 15, 119
Barnes, William (brother), 7, 8, 9, 48, 153
Beauffre, Gen, 166
Begin, Menachem, 129, 130
Bellingham, P. van, 40
Ben Gurion, David, 127
Benn, Tony, 49
Berlin, Sir Isaiah, 76, 132
Bernhard, Prince, 145

Berry, Michael, *see* Hartwell
Betjeman, Sir John, 22
Bevin, Ernest, 60, 68-70, 90
Biesheuvel, Dr, 128
Birgi, Nuri, 93
Blackwell, Richard, 13
Blunt, Anthony, 32
Bonham-Carter, Lady Violet, 166
Bowie, Bob, 83
Brewster, Daniel, 23
Brooke, Basil, *see* Brookeborough
Brookeborough, Viscount, 51
Brosio, Malio, 100
Brown, George, *see* George-Brown
Brown, Rt Rev Laurence, 17
Bruening, Heinrich, 38
Buchan, Alastair, 13, 99
Buchan-Hepburn, Patrick, 50
Bullock, Alan (Lord), 69
Butler, Prof Sir James, 34-5
Butler, Sir Nevile, 35
Butler, R. A. (Lord), 17, 77, 80-2, 101, 102

Caccia, Harold (Lord), 101, 159
Callaghan, James (Lord), 83, 85-6
Campbell, Brig Lorne, 93
Caradon, Lord, 92
Carey, Most Rev George, 27
Carrington, Lord, 85, 86
Cary, Sir Michael, 13
Caspari, Fritz, 118
Chamoun, Camille, 108, 109, 110
Cheshire, Gp Capt Leonard (Lord), 14
Clore, Sir Charles, 123, 124
Coggan, Lord, 29

173

Cohen, Sir Jack, 124
Cole-King, Susan, 20
Courtneidge, Dame Cecily, 49
Crosland, Anthony, 86
Crossman, Richard, 70, 114

David, Alison, 68
Dayan, Moshe, 128-9
Desborough, Lady, 166
Deutschbein, Prof, 113-14
Docker, Rt Rev Colin, 30
Drabble, Margaret, 25
Dring, William, 162
Drogheda, Earl of, 169

Eban, Aubrey, 32, 80, 83, 84, 128
Eden, Anthony, see Avon
Edgar, William, 53
Elizabeth, The Queen Mother, Queen, 8, 23-4, 148
Ellison, Rt Rev Gerald, 23
Erhard, Ludwig, 98, 115
Eyre, Very Rev Richard, 28

Falkender, Lady, 86
Faure, Edgar, 94
Fenner, L. H., 154
Fielding, Leslie, 42, 100
Firth, Budge, 15, 21, 113
Fischer, Ruth, 66
Fisher of Lambeth, Lord, 18, 93
Fitzgerald, Garret, 86
Foot, Hugh, see Caradon
Frangieh, Hamid, 108
Franks, Oliver (Lord), 62, 73
Fraser, Adm of the Fleet Lord, 92

Gage Brown, Canon, 17
Gaitskell, Hugh, 119, 122
Gaulle, Gen de, 79, 80, 96
Geller, Uri, 133
George-Brown, Lord, 82-5
Gladwyn, Lord, 91
Goddard, Mel (daughter), 32, 119, 156
Goodman, Lord, 132

Gordon-Walker, Patrick (Lord), 82
Gorer, Geoffrey, 18
Gould, Bryan, 100
Grant Robertson, Sir Charles, 169
Grese, Irma, 56
Griffith, Guy, 36
Gromyko, Andrei, 81, 95, 101, 102

Haile Selassie, Emperor, 32-3
Hanson, Brian, 26
Hardy, G. H., 17
Harrison, Ernest, 34
Hartwell, Lord, 55
Headlam, Rt Rev Arthur, 16
Healey, Denis (Lord), 98
Heath, Sir Edward, 31, 79-80, 101
Henson, Rt Rev Hensley, 11
Herzog, Haim, 44
Heusinger, Gen, 166
Hindenburg, President von, 57
Holtby, Very Rev Robert, 30
Home of the Hirsel, Lord, 79, 80
Hood, Viscount, 95, 165
Horne, Alistair, 75
Horridge, Mr Justice, 158-9
Housman, A. E., 34
Howatch, Susan, 12
Hulbert, Jack, 49
Hurd, Douglas, 88
Hussein, King, 108, 154

Inchyra, Lord, 165-6
Inge, Very Rev W. R., 12, 30
Inverchapel, Lord, 61, 62, 156

Jackson, H. A., 14-15
Jacobson, David, 121
James, M. R., 166
Jebb, Gladwyn, see Gladwyn
Jenkins, Roy (Lord), 83
Johnson, President L. B., 87, 98
Jones, Cheslyn, 28, 29
Joseph, Sir Max, 149
Jowitt, Earl, 71-2

Kastl, Jörg, 38

Kemp, Rt Rev Eric, 20
Kennedy, President John F., 96, 171-2
Kennedy, Robert, 99
Kilmuir, Earl of, 79
King, Ben, 46
Kirkpatrick, Sir Ivone, 170
Kissin, Harry & Ruth, 163
Kissinger, Henry, 37, 128
Kok, Archbishop, 24
Kollek, Teddy, 27-8, 129
Krupp, Gustav, 55, 114
Kruschev, Nikita, 37, 96, 101, 102
Kuznetsov, V., 101

Lang, Most Rev Cosmo Gordon, 11-12
Leeson, Rt Rev Spencer, 15-16
Leggett, Francie, see Margesson
Lewin, Adm of the Fleet Lord, 149
Lindsay, Lady, 65-6
Littlewood, J. E., 16-17
Lloyd, Selwyn, see Selwyn-Lloyd
Luns, Joseph, 94-5, 146

McCloy, Jack, 98
MacDermot, Lord, 79
Maclean, Donald, 60, 62
Macmillan, Harold, see Stockton
Major, Dr E. D. A., 18
Makarios, Archbishop, 77
Makins, Roger, see Sherfield
Mancroft, Lord, 17, 121
Mann, William, 113
Margesson, Mrs David, 9, 66, 67
Marshall, Gen George, 60, 72
Martin, Paul, 98
Meier-Graefe, Julius, 113
Meir, Golda, 37, 127-8
Menderes, M., 78
Menuhin, Sir Yehudi, 149
Molotov, V. M., 61
Montagu of Beaulieu, Lord, 161
Montefiore, Rt Rev Hugh, 155
Montgomery of Alamein, Field-Marshal Viscount, 52, 56, 166

Moore, Mary, 100
Morrison, Herbert (Lord), 70-2, 73, 74-7
Mountbatten of Burma, Earl, 87, 97, 110, 160

Newman, Cardinal, 32
Niebuhr, Ursula, 28
Nureyev, Rudolf, 168

Oesterreicher, Gusti, 113, 102
Owen, David (Lord), 86

Palliser, Sir Michael, 102
Poynton, John, 15
Presland, Patricia (daughter), 23, 119, 121, 133, 148, 156

Rattigan, Sir Terence, 46
Raven, Canon C. E., 12, 30
Ray, Cyril, 149
Reindorp, Rt Rev George, 26
Revell-Smith, Maj-Gen W. R., 52
Rice-Davies, Mandy, 133
Richardson, Sybil, 162
Robertson, Malcolm, 15
Robinson, C. E., 15
Robinson, Rt Rev John, 16, 22
Rothschild, Jacob (Lord), 43, 44
Rothschild, Mrs James de, 43, 44
Rothschild, Victor (Lord), 42, 43, 155
Rowe, Max, 43
Runcie, Most Rev Robert, 13, 28, 29

Sapir, Pintas, 129
Sargent, Sir Orme, 58
Sassoon, Sarah (daughter), 17, 119, 125, 156
Satterthwaite, Rt Rev John, 22, 23
Saud, King, 110
Savage, Nigel, 41
Schmidt, Helmut, 99
Schuster, Arthur, 121
Schwarzenberg, Prince, 24-5
Scott, Sir Kenneth, 100

Seeds, Sir William, 46
Seligman, Olivia, 80
Seferiades, George, 93
Selwyn-Lloyd, Lord, 77-9
Semeonov, V., 101-2
Shackleton, Lord, 70
Shawcross, Lord, 73
Sherfield, Lord, 73
Sieff, Lord, 123, 124
Simpson, F. A., 34
Slessor, Marshal of the RAF Sir John, 92
Slim, Field-Marshal Viscount, 73, 92
Soames, Christopher (Lord), 48, 85
Soames, Mary (Lady), 48
Spence, Sir Basil, 48
Springer, Sir Hugh, 22-3, 38
Stalin, Joseph, 47, 52, 59, 61-2, 66, 108
Stewart, Michael (Lord), 82
Stikker, Dirk, 146
Stockton, Earl of, 69, 74-7, 78, 79, 96
Stockwood, Very Rev Mervyn, 22
Stopford, Very Rev Robert, 20
Storr, Anthony, 8
Storrs, Peter, 9
Storrs, Sir Ronald, 9
Straight, Michael Whitney, 32
Strang, Lord, 67, 71, 85
Sykes, Sir Richard, 26, 141

Talbot, Matilda, 90
Talbot, Rt Rev Neville, 16
Tappouni, Cardinal, 19
Temple, Most Rev William, 11, 170
Thatcher, Margaret (Lady), 86
Thomson, George (Lord), 98
Thomson, Sir J. J., 33
Timoshenko, Marshal, 52
Tovey, Adm of the Fleet Lord, 54
Trafford, Lord, 87
Treviranus, Gottfried, 66

Truman, President Harry S., 59, 60, 63, 72, 86
Tubman, President, 119

Uchida, Hiro, 38-9

Vacani, Mme, 9
Voroshilov, Marshal, 52

Wagner, Gerrit, 149
Warburg, Sir Siegmund, 13, 123
Ward, Sir A. W. (grandfather), 8, 9, 32, 112, 169
Ward, John (great-grandfather), 58
Watson-Watt, Sir Robert, 18
Webber, Capt, 46
Weizman, Ezer, 83
Weizmann, Chaim, 121, 123
Wellington, Rebecca, 57
Whittaker, R. F. E., 49
Whitworth, Tink, 8
Wijting, Gen Robbie, 146
Wilkinson, Sir Denys, 42
Williams, Rt Rev A. T. P., 15, 16
Williams, Marcia, see Falkender
Willibrands, Cardinal, 255, 158, 160, 165, 167-8, 171
Wilson, Harold (Lord), 82, 86, 87
Wilson, Rt Rev Leonard, 20
Wilson, Rockley, 14
Wilson, Air Marshal Sir Sandy, 170
Winslow, Christa, 113
Winstanley, Denys, 33-4
Wittgenstein, Ludwig, 34
Wolfson, Lord, 123
Woods, Priscilla, 15
Woods, Rt Rev Robin, 21, 27
Wright, Monty, 160

Zorin, V., 101
Zorlu, R., 77-8
Zwartkruis, Bishop, 25